The ROYAL COOKERY BOOK

IN COLOUR

Mrs McKee

Arlington Books
Clifford Street Mayfair
London

THE ROYAL COOKERY BOOK
IN COLOUR
first published 1983 by
Arlington Books (Publishers) Ltd
3 Clifford Street Mayfair
London W1

Text © Mrs McKee 1964 and 1983
Illustrations © Arlington Books 1983

Typeset by Inforum Ltd, Portsmouth
Printed and bound by
Hazell, Watson & Viney Ltd, Aylesbury

British Library Cataloguing in Publication Data
Mrs McKee
The Royal Cookery book in colour.
1. Cookery
I. Title
641.5   TX717

ISBN 0 85140 615 7

FRONTISPIECE: *Fillet of beef with mushrooms and Yorkshire pudding (p. 75)*

Contents

Acknowledgements

————

THE PUBLISHERS ACKNOWLEDGE WITH GRATITUDE THEIR INDEBTEDNESS to the following for their help in the preparation of *The Royal Cookery Book In Colour*:

to Harrods Ltd, Knightsbridge, London, by appointment Suppliers of Provisions and Household Goods, for their unstinting enthusiasm and generosity during the making of this book and for the use of Doulton china tableware, Minton china tableware, Royal Crown Derby china tableware, Paragon china tableware, Spode china tableware, Royal Brierley glassware and all napery;
to Mappin & Webb Ltd, London, by appointment Silversmiths, for all silverware;
to Fortnum & Mason Ltd, Piccadilly, London, by appointment Grocers and Provisions Merchants.

The Publishers would also like to thank Fiona Tillett and Margaret Hall for resplendently re-creating and presenting the recipes, which were illustrated by the talented camera of Marcus Wilson-Smith.

List of Colour Plates

The
ROYAL
COOKERY
BOOK

IN COLOUR

Mrs McKee

Introduction

HOW STRANGE IT IS TO LOOK BACK AND REALISE THAT YOU HAVE
devoted most of your life to food.

Yet cooking is a large part of most women's lives. To some it is a
chore and to others it brings pleasure. I enjoyed cooking as a child in
Sweden because, on a simple level, I found that here was a way to please
people and make them happy. I leave it to others to rhapsodise about the
art of cooking. To me it is an expression of love and care. I think most
women will know what I mean.

Male chefs in the great houses I have known, produce masterpieces of
haute cuisine – magnificent in every way. But if you do not happen to like
a particular dish, then that is considered to be your bad taste. However,
your enjoyment of the food is not really the point: is it, or is it not, a
masterpiece, the chef queries anxiously? Whether or not you actually
like it, is another matter. This, I think, is the essential difference between
the male and female approach to cooking. A man cooks with his head, a
woman with her heart.

I was lucky in the way I learned about cooking. When I was a young
girl, I trained in a huge, beautiful castle in Sweden. The estate was
entirely self-supporting. The animals were slaughtered, salted and
frozen, and we learned how to use every part of a pig or a bullock. We
celebrated a good harvest and prayed against drought and frost; we
knew when the first fruits and vegetables were ripe for picking and
bottling; we were able to cope with last-minute parties for fifty people;
we were toasted in champagne when our food was good and we were
told to throw it away and start again when it was wrong.

I have been lucky, too, in that the people for whom I have cooked
have enjoyed my sort of food, and by so doing they have given me
much happiness in return.

I have never had ambitions beyond wishing to please people with my cooking, and the fact that I have achieved this with Her Majesty the Queen and her family, has been an honour in the deepest sense of the word.

When I first went to cook for Her Majesty, then still the Princess Elizabeth, at Clarence House in 1951, I was told that I was the only female chef in charge of a royal kitchen. I had previously cooked for King Peter of Yugoslavia and his wife, but that was different; they were very young at the time I was with them and very informal. Like most Swedes, I was horribly shy, and on that first day at Clarence House, extremely nervous. I knew deep down that I could manage the job and that hundreds, if not thousands of people had enjoyed my food. But occasionally you might meet someone who happens not to like your style of cooking. There is nothing you can really do about it. Everybody has their own approach – and at fifty-five it was too late to change mine. I prayed I would not have to try.

With my first meal came the first royal compliment. It was to be the forerunner of many, for Her Majesty is one of the most appreciative people for whom I have ever worked. Frequently she would send messages of congratulation or thank me personally after a special dinner. There is something quite riveting about her smile, and I can assure you that when that smile is levelled at you personally, there is nothing you would not do for her.

Perhaps because Her Majesty is such a very inspiring person, I felt that my cooking was at its best during those carefree days at Clarence House, when Prince Charles was just a little boy of four and Princess Anne a tiny, porcelain-skinned baby. As I used to work in a clean white overall every day, Prince Charles called me the lady in white. A nickname that subsequently caught on with the press.

I had never opened a recipe book and I cooked, as always, by taste, adjusting the flavour as I went along. The ideas flowed and I soon ceased to worry that perhaps in one day I would be cooking lunch for four Queens, followed by a dinner party in the evening at which every guest was royal.

It would be naive to imagine that royalty always dine off rare delicacies, though people are sometimes surprised when I go to the trouble of describing how to cook a good kipper or haddock which the Royal Family certainly enjoyed. Perhaps it is because the Royal Family, of all people, have no need to impress that everything is judged on merit alone. In my time at Clarence House, stuffed cabbage received as much appreciation as pheasant or grouse. More, in fact, as the estates at Balmoral and Sandringham were always overflowing with game.

When I first came over from Sweden between the wars and married a Scotsman, people were still eating seven-course meals in the grander houses. But by the time I went to Clarence House, it was only on rare occasions that the Royal Family had five courses. Usually it was not more than three, and the food was good, but simple.

When King George died and Her Majesty eventually moved to Buckingham Palace, I stayed behind at Clarence House to cook for the Queen Mother and Princess Margaret. Before leaving, the Queen asked me to write down a selection of my recipes. As I was not accustomed to making notes of exact weights and measurements, nor to describing my method of cooking in English – I still wrote in Swedish – my instructions were decidedly sketchy. In fact, I felt very sorry for the chef whose job it would be to decipher them.

When Her Majesty reads this book, I would like to offer my profoundest apologies.

For a time at Clarence House, I was flattered to find that my name as a chef was becoming known. By this I mean that it was known to the small circle of top calibre chefs who were employed by the few remaining, large, private households, or who worked for clubs and distinguished restaurants. These chefs, all men, invited me to dinner and, in turn, produced their masterpieces, generously giving me the recipes. I asked them back and gave of my best. It was all very jolly until I was asked for my 'secrets'. Sooner than reveal that I had only the vaguest idea of how much of this or that I put into a dish, I preserved a mysterious silence. And that was the end of the dinner parties!

After this, and the inadequate recipes I was forced to give to the Queen, I started studying myself at work in the kitchen, and for the first time began weighing things and analysing my methods. The result is the recipes in this book.

Perhaps the best advice I can give to anyone who wants to make others happy with their cooking, is to cook with love and trust your palate. Taste the food as you go along and do not be afraid to adjust the flavour according to your own palate. Due to the temperature, season and type of storage, food is susceptible to a hundred and one variations.

As for love – no dish should be served without it.

Many people helped me in compiling this book. I shall start, properly enough, by thanking my husband. Not so much, however, for his inspiration but for the way he resigned himself to eating six ill-assorted test recipes in one evening and his practical help in cooking his own bacon and eggs on most others, when I was too busy writing about food to cook it.

I also thank Miss Maureen Owen for her valuable assistance, and all the other people who helped us both. In particular, Miss Grace Fisk, who kept the children out of our hair; Mr Jones the butcher and Mr Cross the grocer, who brought us out odd items after their shops were shut; Mrs Longhurst, Mrs Goodwin, Mrs Bromley and Mrs Smith, who kept up a human chain of help in the house; Mrs Doris Rose, who came to the rescue with her clear English handwriting when everyone went on strike against my indecipherable Swedish script. And many thanks, too, to the neighbours who took in laundry and bread, but held back on visits and gossip until they knew we could do them justice.

Soups

WHAT TO SERVE AS AN ORIGINAL FIRST COURSE CAN BE A PROBLEM, BUT the solution is very often simple: a thoroughly good soup.

The *good* soup is the one you make in your kitchen. Packets and tins are no substitute for the love and care you can put into a soup. It is a happy dish to make too; the low bubbling and delicious fragrance fills the kitchen with a warm atmosphere of contentment.

Soup is what you make it. It can be grand enough for a banquet, satisfying enough for a hard-working farmer, or creamy and sophisticated enough for the smart set. Soup nourishes the sick, gives strength to the active, and can be served hot or cold in winter or summer. One could hardly have a more versatile dish.

It would be sad if anyone thought of soup as dull, but it can certainly be disappointing if it does not receive its due measure of love and care in the preparation. To obtain the best from many soups it is necessary to let them simmer for several hours. But this should not dishearten anyone for they will simmer along quite happily on their own, and the gentle bubbling provides a cheerful background noise.

In Sweden we pay a lot of attention to soup garnishes as we think that a good soup deserves something rather special to mark the occasion. You will find some unusual garnishes in this chapter which will, I hope, arouse your interest and encourage you to think of other accompaniments to serve.

For the warmer weather, cold soups are very popular, and there can be no more soothing start to a meal on a hot summer's evening.

In writing this chapter I was reminded particularly of Princess Margaret, Prince Charles and ex-Queen Alexandra of Yugoslavia – all great soup people. Queen Alexandra was my chief soup patron, and for her I would rack my brains for a different soup each evening; the more adventurous they were, the more she liked them. With Princess Margaret I took great trouble to produce a classic, elegant sort of soup, and Prince Charles just thought that soup was great fun.

And I, for one, wholeheartedly agree with him.

The best of all good soups is the clear consommé. It does take time, admittedly, but in that time all the goodness from the meat and vegetables is extracted and you have a wonderful, nutritious soup at the end.

CLEAR CONSOMMÉ

To make about 4 pints/2.5 litres:

3 lbs/1.5 Kg shin of beef	½ stick of celery
1½ lbs/750 g shin of veal	1 onion
6 pints/3.5 litres water	1 bay leaf
2 teaspoons of salt	sprig of parsley
1 carrot	sprig of thyme
1 leek	4 or 5 peppercorns
½ beetroot	1 clove
1 parsnip	

Cut the meat up and break the bones. Rinse well and place in a saucepan. Cover with the water and allow to stand for one hour. Add the salt and bring to the boil over a low heat. Spoon the scum from the surface, then add the vegetables, cleaned and peeled but not cut. Add the herbs tied in a bundle, the peppercorns and the clove. Bring up to the boil again slowly and simmer for five or six hours on a low heat in an open pan.

When cooked, remove the meat and vegetables and strain the consommé through a colander lined with dampened muslin. Remove any remaining grease from the surface of the consommé with a paper towel. Serve hot or cold.

CLEAR CHICKEN CONSOMMÉ

To make about 4 pints/2.5 litres:

1 large boiling fowl (about 5 lbs/2.5 Kg)	1 onion
	1 bay leaf
2 ozs/60 g butter	sprig of thyme
½ lb/250 g shin of veal	sprig of parsley
½ lb/250 g shin of beef	1 teaspoon of salt
10 peppercorns	1 stick of celery
1 clove	1 leek

Remove the chicken breast and chop bones and legs in pieces. Remove skin and rinse well. Dry thoroughly. Brown the butter in a saucepan, add the chicken and brown over a low heat until golden. Pour in enough water to cover the chicken and bring slowly to the boil. Meanwhile, put the veal and beef, cut in large pieces, in a stock pot with water to cover and let stand for half an hour. Remove the scum from the chicken stock, add it to the meat and bring to the boil very gently, skimming the surface from time to time. Add the peppercorns and the clove stuck into an onion, herbs and one teaspoon of salt. Add all the vegetables, peeled but uncut and bring to the boil slowly. Simmer for at least three hours in an open pan.

Strain the consommé through a colander lined with dampened muslin. Serve hot or cold.

Once you have gone to the trouble of making these superlative consommés you will want to use them in a variety of different ways.

Now follow some very special soups with a consommé base, which will add enormous prestige to your reputation for keeping a good table.

CONSOMMÉ DE VOLAILLE AUX POINTS D'ASPERGES

To serve 6:

2 chicken breasts	1 glass of sherry
2 pints/1.25 litres good chicken consommé (see previous recipe)	seasoning to taste
	2 tablespoons of chopped fresh parsley
small tin of asparagus tips	

Cut the chicken breasts in small pieces and place them in a pan with enough water to cover them. Add salt and boil on a gentle heat, spooning off any scum that rises to the surface, until tender. Strain the stock from the chicken breasts and add it to the consommé. Add the chicken pieces and the asparagus tips with the juice from the tin. Add the sherry, season to taste and, just before serving, add the chopped parsley. Serve hot but do not boil.

CONSOMMÉ RIS DE VEAU AUX PETITS POIS VERT

To serve 6:

½ lb/250 g calves' sweetbreads
1½ pints/90 cl clear consommé
  (for recipe see page 16)
1 lb/500 g fresh or frozen peas
pinch of sugar

1 fresh or tinned truffle, peeled
  and finely chopped
1 glass of white wine
salt and pepper to taste

This consommé is definitely a tiara event, but one that you should enjoy even without the tiara. It will go a lovely green colour.

Soak the sweetbreads in cold water, then blanch in boiling water for about two minutes. Peel off the surface membrane and any fat or gristle, and press under a board for about two hours to compact the flesh. Place the pressed sweetbreads in a pan, add enough water to cover and braise for about 30 to 40 minutes. Cut into small pieces and then add to the consommé. Cook the peas in salted water with a pinch of sugar for about five minutes, being careful not to overcook. Strain and add to the consommé. Add the wine, the chopped truffle and, if using a tinned truffle, the juice from the tin. Season with salt and pepper and serve hot.

PETITE MARMITE

To serve 6:

2 pints/1.25 litres clear
  consommé (for recipe see
  page 16)

the cooked vegetables used in
  making the consommé
1 glass of sherry

For the bread croutons:
3 slices of stale white bread

2 ozs/60 g butter

Skim all fat from the cooled consommé and then press the cooked vegetables through a fine sieve to obtain a smooth purée. Add the purée to the soup with a glass of sherry. Heat the soup gently but do not boil. While the soup is heating make the bread croutons. Remove the crusts from the bread, and cut it into small cubes. Melt the butter in a sauté pan over a low heat and gently fry the bread cubes until they are crisp all the way through, and golden brown. Serve the hot croutons with the soup either separately or as a garnish.

Here are some consommés with unusual garnishes. They make exciting soups for special occasions.

GAME CONSOMMÉ WITH CREAM OF CHICKEN AND TRUFFLE

To serve 6:

game carcasses, for making the stock	1 carrot
3 pints/1.75 litres cold water	2 onions, peeled and cut
10 white peppercorns	1 bay leaf
1 tablespoon of salt	sprig of parsley

For the garnish:

2 breasts of boiling chickens	pinch of sugar
2 whites of eggs	1 truffle, peeled and finely
$\frac{1}{2}$ pint/30 cl double cream	chopped
salt and pepper to taste	lettuce

Braise the game carcasses in the oven for half an hour. Place them in a saucepan and cover with about 3 pints/1.75 litres of cold water. Bring slowly to the boil and remove all scum. Add the seasoning, vegetables and herbs and simmer for four to five hours. Strain and remove all fat. Keep hot.

To make the garnish, mince the chicken breasts three times and mix with the raw whites of eggs. Stir in the cream gradually. Add salt, pepper and the sugar. Stir for fifteen minutes and add the truffle. Shape mixture into small balls with a teaspoon and boil in the consommé for a few minutes.

Pour the consommé into cups, add the chicken and truffle balls, and just before serving cut a lettuce into strips and use to garnish.

CONSOMMÉ WITH BOUCHÉES MIMOSA

To serve 6:

For the consommé:

2 pints/1.25 litres game consommé (see previous recipe)

1 truffle, peeled and cut into strips (optional)
1 glass of port wine

For the bouchées mimosa:

8 small puff pastry cases
1 large tin of asparagus tips
1 tablespoon of plain flour
¼ pint/15 cl double cream
1 oz/30 g butter

pepper, salt and a pinch of sugar to taste
4 hard-boiled eggs
1 oz/30 g Parmesan cheese, grated

This recipe is more than just soup; the garnish is more than just an ordinary garnish. Together they make a delicious first course.

Heat the consommé and add the wine and truffle. Put the *bouchée* cases into a low oven to heat. Strain the asparagus juice into a saucepan, add the flour and whisk until smooth. Bring to the boil stirring all the time and simmer for ten minutes. Add the cream and the butter and season to taste. Chop the white of the hard-boiled eggs coarsely and cut the asparagus tips each to about one inch in length. Add asparagus tips and chopped egg white to the sauce, then the Parmesan cheese. Heat, but do not boil.

Fill the *bouchées* with the mixture. Sieve the yolks of eggs over the *bouchées* and serve hot with the consommé.

CONSOMMÉ ROYAL

Pre-heat oven to 150°C/300°F or gas mark 2
To serve 6:

2 pints/1.25 litres beef consommé

salt and a pinch of sugar

For the egg royal garnish:

1 egg
3 egg yolks
7 fl oz/20 cl single cream
pinch of nutmeg

1 sweet red pepper, sliced
  thinly
2 tomatoes peeled, seeded and
  cut in strips

Here is a rather grand soup, made from the best beef consommé, that I often served at Clarence House on special occasions. The garnish melts in the mouth and is quite delicious. It looks very good too and always attracted favourable comment.

Gently heat the beef consommé, add seasoning and while it is heating make the garnish. Whisk the eggs and egg yolks together with the cream, and add the nutmeg. Grease a soufflé dish or small metal moulds with butter and pour in the mixture. Place the custards on a grill set in a tin and pour in enough hot water to come halfway up the sides of the moulds. Cover the tin and poach in the oven pre-heated to 150°C/300°F or gas mark 2 for fifteen to twenty minutes, or until set. When cold turn out and cut in small diamond shapes.

Garnish the hot soup with the egg royal, the red pepper and tomato.

CONSOMMÉ CONTESSA

To serve 4:

1 tin of asparagus tips
4 ozs/125 g cooked ox tongue
1½ pints/90 cl clear chicken
  consommé (for recipe see
  page 16)

4 ozs/125 g tapioca
1 glass of sherry
salt and pepper to taste

Cut the asparagus tips in half and cut the tongue into strips. Put the consommé in a saucepan and bring to a gentle boil. Add the tapioca and simmer for fifteen minutes. Add the asparagus tips together with the juice from the tin, the wine and the tongue. Make very hot, taste, season with the salt and pepper and serve.

CONSOMMÉ EN GELÉE AUX SHERRY

To serve 6:

2 pints/1.25 litres clear consommé (for recipe see page 16)
1 glass of sherry or white wine

salt and pepper to taste
chopped sweet red or green pepper or parsley for decoration

Add to the consommé the glass of sherry or white wine and adjust seasoning to taste. Serve with chopped red or green pepper or parsley for decoration.

CONSOMMÉ BALMORAL AUX HOMARD

To serve 6:

1 × 1 lb/500 g cooked lobster or tinned lobster
½ lb/250 g cooked sweetbreads
1 oz/30 g butter
1 tablespoon of brandy
½ pint/30 cl of tomato purée
½ clove of garlic
3 ozs/90 g shallots
¼ pint/15 cl dry white wine
2 small sprigs of tarragon

salt and cayenne pepper, to taste
2 pints/1.25 litres hot fish stock (for recipe see page 221)
2 egg yolks
¼ pint/15 cl double cream
2 tablespoons of grated Gruyère cheese

Making a fish consommé is not the difficult task many people imagine it to be. A good fish stock is essential, however. The fish used for making the stock must be fresh and of good quality. You will find my recipe for fish stock on page 221.

Cut the cooked lobster in half lengthways and remove the meat, taking care not to use the little bag near the head. Cut the meat into small pieces leaving aside some for garnishing. Put the lobster into a saucepan with the cut, cooked sweetbreads and add the butter. Stir until hot, then add the brandy and set it alight. Pour in the tomato purée, the garlic, shallots, the wine, tarragon and seasoning, and bring to the boil.

Cover the saucepan and simmer for ten minutes. Remove from the heat and allow to cool.

Press the mixture through a sieve with a wooden pestle. Discard the residual solids and place the liquid in a saucepan with the hot fish stock. Stir well and bring to the boil. Check the seasoning and strain the soup once more.

Heat, remove from cooker, beat up the egg yolks with the cream and then stir into the soup. Add the pieces of lobster and the grated cheese. Stir and heat well, but do not boil. Serve immediately.

This soup is also delicious cold, but omit the cheese.

OYSTER SOUP

To serve 6:

1 tablespoon of cornflour	2 egg yolks
3 pints/1.75 litres fish stock	$\frac{1}{4}$ pint/15 cl white wine
(for recipe see page 221)	1 tablespoon grated Parmesan
12 live oysters	cheese
salt and pepper to taste	$\frac{1}{2}$ sweet green pepper, finely
1 oz/30 g butter	chopped

For the garnish:
veal and chicken frikadellers
   (for recipe see page 93)

Mix the cornflour with a little fish stock, and stir until smooth. Bring the fish stock to the boil and thicken with the cornflour, stir well and simmer for five minutes. Remove from heat.

Open the oysters by prising the shells apart with the blade of an oyster knife. Strain the juice from the oysters into a small saucepan and remove the oyster beards. Place the saucepan over a high heat, boil up and remove at once. Strain the oyster juice into the thickened fish stock, add the seasoning and the butter. Beat the egg yolks together with the wine in a cup of the hot soup. Add to the soup and whisk well. Keep hot, but do not boil.

Remove the oysters from their shells and add them to the pan. Put a lid on the pan and keep hot for five to ten minutes, but do not boil as this will toughen the oysters. Stir in the grated cheese. Pour into soup bowls and sprinkle a teaspoon of chopped pepper into each plate.

If adding the frikadellers, make the mixture according to the recipe and then poach them in boiling fish stock. Cover with a lid and simmer for five minutes. When cooked, add them to the soup with the cheese.

FISH SOUP À LA RUSSE

To serve 4:

1 lb/500 g cod or haddock	salt and pepper
1 onion	juice of $\frac{1}{2}$ lemon
1 carrot	$\frac{1}{4}$ pint/15 cl white wine
sprig of parsley	1 tablespoon of sweet green
1 clove	pepper, chopped
1 teaspoon of Marmite	24 oysters
$\frac{1}{2}$ a bay leaf	2 tablespoons of chopped fresh
1$\frac{1}{2}$ pints/90 cl water	parsley

For the cheese canapés:

white bread, sliced	1 egg white, whipped
butter	dash of Cayenne pepper
$\frac{1}{4}$ lb/125 g grated Gruyére cheese	

Clean and cut up the fish leaving in the bone and put in a saucepan with the onion, carrot, parsley, clove, pepper, Marmite, the bay leaf and the water. Bring to the boil over a high heat and then simmer for about twenty-five minutes or until the fish is broken up. Strain off the stock through a dampened muslin cloth, replace the stock in the saucepan and add seasoning to taste. Heat and add the lemon juice, wine and the pepper.

Remove the beards from the oysters and put them in a small saucepan with their juice. Bring to the boil quickly and remove at once. Strain the juice into the soup. Make the soup very hot, without actually boiling. It should have turned a golden brown colour. Remove the pan from the heat, add the oysters, cover with a lid and allow to stand for ten minutes. Add the chopped parsley.

Consommé ris de veau au petits pois vert (p. 18)

For a splendid accompaniment to this soup, try cheese canapés.

Spread slices of white bread with butter and cut into fingers. Mix ¼ lb/125 g grated Gruyère cheese with whipped white of egg and a dash of cayenne pepper. Spread on the bread and bake in a hot oven until golden brown. Salted biscuits or cream crackers can be used instead of bread.

CREAM OF PEAS MONACO

To serve 4:

1 lb/500 g fresh green peas	1 oz/30 g butter
2 pints/1.25 litres beef stock	chopped mint
½ pint/30 cl double cream	1 tablespoon of sweet red
pepper, salt and pinch of sugar	pepper, cut in small pieces
to season	

This is a delicious creamy soup. First, cook the peas in salted water. Strain and sieve. Add the peas to the hot beef stock together with the cream, sugar and pepper and salt to taste. Heat thoroughly, but do not boil, then remove the pan from the heat and whisk in the butter. Garnish with chopped mint and red pepper.

CREAM ALEXANDRA

To serve 4:

2 ozs/60 g butter	the breast of a cooked chicken,
2 ozs/60 g plain flour	minced and sieved
2 pints/1.25 litres chicken stock	

For the garnish:

¼ pint/15 cl single cream	1 carrot cut in fine strips and
½ teacup of petit pois cooked in salted water	cooked in chicken stock

Here is another soup much liked by ex-Queen Alexandra of Yugoslavia

Cold consommé with oysters (p. 31)

– a great soup person. It is very smooth and creamy with quite an exciting flavour.

Melt the butter and stir in the flour. Add the heated stock and stir until smooth. Bring to the boil, stirring all the time and boil for ten minutes. Add the minced chicken breast and simmer for a further ten minutes. Remove from the cooker. Heat, but do not boil the cream and add the peas and carrots. Pour into the soup, season to taste and serve.

ROSA'S COCKIE LEEKIE

To serve 6:

1 boiling chicken	¼ lb/125 g cooked and stoned
a little bacon	prunes
veal or beef bones (cooked)	1½ lb/750 g chopped and partly
salt and pepper	cooked leeks

For a good, warming winter supper there is nothing better than a dish of hearty soup. It is a complete meal.

Rosa's Cockie Leekie is a traditional Scottish recipe – good and hearty with a whole fowl which is left to simmer all day. The recipe was sent to me by a Scotswoman, who got it, she says, from Rosa Maltravers, cook to the noble Forbes family of Aberdeenshire for twenty-one years. Rosa, a fine Scottish cook, was famous for her Cockie Leekie, and one cannot do better than follow her version which is essentially a simple soup, calling for no special preparations.

First, cover the fowl, bones and bacon with water in a saucepan and leave to simmer all day. Season to taste. Strain the fowl and its stock through a sieve. Add the prunes and the leeks cut in half-inch squares to the stock. Return to the stove to heat thoroughly. Finally, add chopped meat from the fowl, if desired, and serve piping hot.

NETTLE SOUP WITH EGG BALLS (*Nessel Kal*)

To serve 4:

1 pint/60 cl good stock made from veal and pork bones	1 tablespoon of plain flour
	pepper, salt and a pinch of sugar to season

½ pint/30 cl nettle tops, cooked
    and puréed through a fine
    sieve

½ tablespoon of finely-chopped
    chives
1 tablespoon of cold butter

For the egg balls:
2 hard-boiled eggs
½ oz/15 g butter

1 tablespoon of grated Gruyère
    cheese

If you have a garden with a stinging nettle problem, don't despair – eat them. In Sweden, nettle soup is quite a delicacy. The nettle tops have a light, delicious taste rather like asparagus. They are said to help cure rheumatism too! Snip off tender nettle tops in April or early May, cook them for approximately five minutes and then sieve.

Bring the stock to the boil and thicken with the flour diluted in a little water. Simmer for ten minutes. Add the seasoning and sugar, the sieved nettles and the chives. Simmer for twenty minutes. Remove from heat, add the butter and stir with a whisk. Keep warm.

To make the egg balls, remove the yolks of the hard-boiled eggs and mix with the butter and cheese to form a smooth cream. Let the mixture harden a little in a cool place, then roll into small balls. The egg balls can be made while the soup is simmering so that they are ready to float in the soup just before serving.

In Sweden we sometimes make a meal of *nessel kal* by serving poached eggs sprinkled with Parmesan cheese instead of the egg balls.

SWEDISH KOTTSOPPA

To serve 6–8:

2 lbs/1 Kg chuck rib of beef
2 lbs/1 Kg silverside of beef
6½ pints/ 4 litres water
2 teaspoons of salt
10 white peppercorns
a sprig of thyme
1 bay leaf

2 onions cut in halves
2 carrots
1 parsnip
1 stick of celery
1 leek
a sprig of parsley

Kottsoppa is the Swedish version of pot au feu, and is served in Sweden as a substantial supper dish with boiled potatoes and horseradish sauce.

Put the meat in a deep saucepan with the water and bring to the boil slowly. Remove any scum, add salt, peppercorns, herbs, onions, one of the carrots and the parsnip. Cover the saucepan and simmer for three to four hours. When the meat is cooked, strain half the amount of stock into another saucepan and remove fat. Cut all the remaining vegetables into thin strips and add to the strained stock. Simmer until the vegetables are cooked. Add chopped parsley.

The meat should be sliced and served with plain boiled potatoes, with horseradish sauce made with the remaining stock from the meat.

POTAGE INTERLAKEN

To serve 4:

2 chicken breasts	$\frac{1}{4}$ pint/15 cl double cream
2 pints/1.25 litres good chicken stock	1 oz/30 g grated Parmesan cheese
4 ozs/125 g of noodles	pepper and a pinch of sugar to taste
1 egg	

This is a good, satisfying soup from Switzerland which I once enjoyed in Interlaken. You cut the chicken breasts into small pieces and boil them in enough salted water to cover them. Heat the chicken stock and cook the noodles. Beat the egg with the cream. Remove the stock from the heat and whisk in the egg and cream mixture. Add the chopped up chicken and the cooked noodles, season to taste and sprinkle in the cheese.

Serve hot, but do not boil once the egg mixture has been added.

MEAT SOUP WITH BARLEY

To serve 6:

2 lbs/1 Kg shin of beef with bone	2 chicken stock cubes
	1 carrot

1 parsnip
1½ tablespoons of pearl barley
1 stick of celery
2 leeks cut in rings

salt and pepper
½ lb/250 g small potatoes
parsley

Cut the meat into squares and chop up the bones. Put into a saucepan together with enough water to cover, add salt and bring slowly to the boil. Remove scum and simmer for an hour. Dissolve chicken cubes in a little water and add to the meat stock together with the peeled and cut vegetables and barley. Season, cover the pan and bring to the boil. Simmer for two hours.

Fifteen minutes before cooking time is up, add the peeled potatoes. When ready, scoop out bones and fat and add freshly-chopped parsley.

POTAGE ALEXANDRA

To serve 6:

2½ ozs/75 g butter
2 tablespoons of plain flour
2 pints/1.25 litres of chicken
    stock
salt, pepper and sugar to taste
2 ozs/60 g noodles, blanched

¾ pint/45 cl milk
20 prawns for garnishing
¼ pint/15 cl double cream
dash of cayenne pepper
2 tablespoons of Gruyère
    cheese

This soup was not in fact created for Princess Alexandra but for ex-Queen Alexandra of Yugoslavia, for whom I worked at one time. She adored it, but ex-King Peter only liked clear consommé and they used to eat different soups at dinner.

Melt 2 ozs/60 g of butter in a saucepan. Add the flour, mix well and stir in the heated stock a little at a time. Stir until smooth and creamy. Season. Bring to the boil and simmer over a gentle heat for ten minutes.

Meanwhile cut the blanched noodles into slices and boil in the milk until tender, adding more milk if necessary. Add the cream, cayenne pepper, cheese and the rest of the butter. Do not boil.

ROSE HIP SOUP WITH CREAM

To serve 4:

1 pint/500 g rose hips
3 pints/1.75 litres water
¼ lb/125 g sugar
small cup of sultanas
2 tablespoons of cornflour

1 tablespoon of blanched
  almonds
½ pint/30 cl whipped double
  cream

Rose hips are the orange-red, oval berries of the wild rose, found on the bushes between late August and November. They are not cultivated and are not available in the shops.

Boil the rose hips in water for one and a half hours, stirring frequently and mashing with a fork. When cooked, pass them through a fine sieve. Put the sieved rose hips into a clean pan, add the sugar and the sultanas, previously washed in hot water. Bring to the boil and remove any scum. Reduce the heat. Mix the cornflour with half a cup of cold water and whisk into the soup. Boil for two minutes. Remove from the heat and add the almonds cut into strips. Allow to cool.

Serve cold with a spoonful of whipped cream in each cup.

GELÉE EN MELON

To serve 4:

½ pint/30 cl white wine
1 tablespoon of tomato purée
1½ pints/90 cl good beef
  consommé

1 honeydew melon
5 ozs/150 g ham, cut in thin
  strips

Mix the wine and tomato purée with the heated consommé, and then allow to cool almost to setting point. Cut the melon in half and remove seeds. Scoop out the melon flesh with a teaspoon so that it resembles small eggs and put in individual soup cups. Spoon the consommé over them and sprinkle the ham on top. Chill and serve cold.

COLD CONSOMMÉ WITH OYSTERS

To serve 4:

1½ pints/90 cl reduced chicken
   consommé (for recipe see
   page 16)
1 glass of dry white wine

30 oysters
shredded lettuce
lemon slices, to garnish

Heat the consommé and mix in the white wine. Remove the beards from the oysters and put the oysters with their juice in a small saucepan and bring to the boil. Remove at once and add the oysters and juice to the consommé. Cool and allow to set to a jelly.

   Serve in glasses with strips of lettuce in the bottom. Garnish with lemon twists.

COLD TOMATO SOUP WITH CUCUMBER

To serve 4:

12 tomatoes
1 onion
1 oz/30 g butter
1½ pints/90 cl water

seasoning
1 glass of Madeira
2 teaspoons of cornflour
½ cucumber

Rinse and slice the tomatoes in quarters. Chop the onion finely and braise lightly in the butter. Add the tomatoes, seasoning and the water. Bring to the boil and simmer for twenty minutes until the tomatoes are mushy. Pass through a fine sieve to remove seeds and skins, add the Madeira and bring to the boil.

   Dissolve the cornflour in a little water and stir into the soup with a whisk. Boil for five minutes, then remove from heat and cool. Peel the cucumber and cut into pieces, removing the seeds. Add the cucumber to the tomato soup and serve chilled in soup cups.

   To garnish, you could add some good cream cheese piped in the centre of each cup or serve cheese crisps separately.

GELÉE DE VOLAILLE AU TOMATES

To serve 4:

½ lb/250 g raw minced shin of beef
2 onions, peeled and cut in rings
½ sweet red pepper, seeded and cut in slices
2 whites of egg
8 tomatoes cut in quarters

salt and pepper to taste
10 white peppercorns
¼ teaspoon of garlic salt
½ teaspoon of celery salt
4 pints/2.5 litres good chicken consommé (for recipe see page 16)
1 hard-boiled egg, to garnish

Place the beef, vegetables, raw egg whites and tomatoes in a saucepan and add the seasoning. Mix over the heat and add the consommé. Bring slowly to the boil and then simmer for one and a quarter hours. Remove from heat and allow to stand for fifteen minutes. Strain through a dampened muslin cloth. The soup should be a clear ruby colour. Cool nearly to setting point and garnish with the hard-boiled egg white, finely chopped, and the sieved yolk.

Chill and serve.

VELOUTÉ DE VOLAILLE FROID

To serve 4:

1 pint/60 cl chicken consommé (for recipe see page 16)
1 pint/60 cl new green peas, puréed
1 egg yolk
¼ pint/15 cl double cream

1 tablespoon of finely chopped mint
pepper, salt and sugar to taste
4 ozs/125 g bacon cut in strips and fried until crisp, to garnish

Heat the consommé in a saucepan, add the purée of peas, stir and bring to the boil. Boil for five minutes, then remove from the heat but keep hot. Beat together the egg yolk and the cream and add to the soup with the mint. Mix well and season to taste. Pour into soup cups to cool. When set, garnish with the bacon strips and serve.

COLD CHERRY SOUP CHANTILLY

To serve 6:

2 ozs/60 g blanched almonds	½ lb/250 g caster sugar
2¼ lbs/1 Kg fresh cherries	4 teaspoons of cornflour
2 pints/1.25 litres water	½ pint/30 cl sweet white wine
1 stick of cinnamon	¼ pint/15 cl double cream

Skin the almonds, cut in strips and toast lightly. Wash and stem the cherries, reserving some to garnish the soup, and put in a saucepan with the water and cinnamon stick. Boil for twenty-five minutes. In the meantime, stone the remaining cherries and put aside for garnishing.

Strain the juice from the cooked cherries into a saucepan, add the sugar and bring to the boil. Add the reserved cherries. Mix the cornflour with half a cup of water and thicken the soup slightly. Mix well with a whisk to prevent lumps. Boil for about two minutes, then remove from heat and add the wine. Serve cold in soup cups with a spoonful of whipped cream on top of each, and sprinkle with the toasted almonds.

Fish

I AM A GREAT FISH-EATER. OF ALL THE RECIPES IN THIS BOOK, THOSE THAT I most enjoy preparing and eating are in this chapter.

I owe much to fish. Its rich source of Vitamin D has helped to sustain my energy and well-being throughout many hectic periods. Almost the first thing I did when moving house was to check that there was a good fishmonger in the area. My ideal place to live would, of course, be in a sea port so that I could buy the fish directly they came out of the sea!

I know that I have been spoilt as regards buying fish, for when I was at Clarence House all the fish came direct from London's Billingsgate Fish Market. Shopping without the Royal Warrant is rather a different matter, as I have subsequently found.

Use your eyes and – very important – your nose to ensure the fish is fresh. How can you be sure? With me it is instinct, but here is how I think I do it. First, look the fish in the eye. If the eyes are bright and clear with what I can only describe as that rather appealing look, it is all right. If you are not sure, cast an eye over the flesh which should be a bluish white, the gills scarlet. If you are still not sure, prod the fish, sniffing hard at the same time. If your finger leaves a dent and there is that unmistakable whiff, buy frozen fish instead.

With shellfish, be doubly careful. You will have to rely very much upon your fishmonger for fresh lobster and crab; frozen, peeled prawns are often preferable to the fresh prawns unless very fresh indeed, and when buying frozen shrimps, buy the larger packets as shrimps in small quantities rarely seem to freeze well.

There should be no snobbery about fish. Every fish possesses its own proud heritage. At the right time of year, salmon or trout are delicious and desirable to buy; at other times a fresh piece of cod is a dish fit for a queen. Indeed, I have often been proud to serve it to Her Majesty. My favourite dish is freshest haddock, dipped in melted butter, lightly floured and grilled.

Shellfish provides a rich variety of excellent dishes and with frozen prawns and shrimps readily available, you can always be sure the fish is fresh. A *good* prawn cocktail calls for judgement and artistry. Once at Clarence House I had an inspiration for a lunch-time party: I whipped the mayonnaise very stiff and coloured one half green and the other half red. I then swirled it around the inside of the glass so as to create a different-coloured ribbon effect before putting in the prawn mixture. Served with crushed ice, it made a cool-looking dish for a summer's afternoon. The luncheon party was most amused.

Mackerel is a fish which, ideally, should be caught and eaten on the same day, but this is not possible, of course, if you live some distance from the coast. I always think of it as a holiday fish because the Royal Family used particularly to like to eat it on holiday at Balmoral where it came straight from the Scottish ports. They were very fond of fish and would have it every day, usually in the evening when a fish course would be served at dinner.

FILLETS OF CODFISH AU GRATIN

Pre-heat oven to 180° C/350°F or gas mark 4
To serve 3–4:

1 lb/500 g cod fillets	4 anchovy fillets
1 oz/30 g butter	$\frac{1}{4}$ pint/15 cl creamy milk
$\frac{1}{2}$ pint/30 cl Scotch egg sauce (for recipe see page 213)	$\frac{1}{2}$ cup grated Parmesan cheese

Rinse the cod fillets, remove skin and bone and dry thoroughly. Cut into fingers about 1 inch thick. Butter a fireproof dish and cover the bottom with a little of the Scotch egg sauce. Place the fillets in the dish, cut the anchovies in pieces and place them on top of the fish. Cover with the rest of the sauce and smooth over with a knife. Dot knobs of butter on top. Pour on the milk and sprinkle with the cheese. Bake in the oven at 180°C/350°F or gas mark 4 for twenty minutes.

Velouté de volaille froid (p. 32)
OVERLEAF, LEFT: *Coquilles St Jacques Balmoral (p. 46)*
OVERLEAF, RIGHT: *Roulades de saumon fumée (p. 47)*

CODFISH PIE

Pre-heat oven to 180°C/350°F or gas mark 4
To serve 4:

2½ ozs/75 g butter
3 anchovy fillets
2 tablespoons of tomato purée
2 lbs/1 Kg potatoes, peeled
1 oz/30 g butter
3 fl ozs/8 cl boiled milk
1 egg yolk

seasoning
1 pint/60 cl Scotch egg sauce
  (for recipe see page 213)
1 lb/500 g cod fillets
1 tablespoon of double cream
1 tablespoon of Parmesan
  cheese, grated

Melt 1½ ozs/40 g of the butter over a low heat, add the anchovies and the tomato purée. Mix well together.

Boil the potatoes in salted water, strain and mash with the remaining butter and then pour in the hot milk gradually. Beat well, then add the egg yolk and seasoning.

Butter a fireproof dish, pour a layer of Scotch egg sauce on the bottom, add the cod fillets and spread the tomato and anchovy mixture on top. Pour over the rest of the Scotch egg sauce. Spread the cream on top. Pipe the creamed potatoes in a pretty pattern on top and sprinkle with cheese.

Bake in the oven at 180°C/350°F or gas mark 4 for twenty minutes until the potato is golden-brown.

FISH CAKES

To make 12 fish cakes

½ lb/250 g cooked cod or
  haddock
salt, pepper and pinch of sugar
½ lb/250 g potatoes, mashed

1 egg, beaten
3 ozs/90 g butter
plain flour

Flake and bone the fish and mix with the seasoning, potato, egg and 1 oz/30 g of the butter. It does not matter if the butter is a bit lumpy. Shape into cakes and roll in flour. Fry slowly in remaining butter until

Saumon court bouillon (p. 50)

golden-brown. This will take quite a long time, as fish cakes need gentle treatment. Dish up and pour butter over the fish cakes.

Delicious served for breakfast with a slice of crisp bacon.

POACHED FRESH HADDOCK IN BUTTER SAUCE

Pre-heat oven to 220°C/425°F or gas mark 7
To serve 3–4:

1 lb/500 g fillet of haddock, fresh or frozen
1 teaspoon of salt
1 oz/30 g butter
½ pint/30 cl milk

½ pint/30 cl English butter sauce (for recipe see page 217)
1 tablespoon of mayonnaise or salad cream
chopped parsley and sweet red or green pepper, to garnish

Rinse and dry the haddock, remove skin and bones. Cut the fillets in portions, sprinkle with the salt, and place in a buttered fireproof dish. Cover with greaseproof paper and poach in milk in the oven at 220°C/425°F or gas mark 7 for twelve–fifteen minutes. If the fillets are frozen they will take nearer twenty minutes.

When cooked, remove to a serving dish. Strain the remains of the juice from the poaching into the butter sauce and add the mayonnaise or salad cream. Heat the sauce, but do not boil. Cover the fish with the sauce and sprinkle with chopped parsley and pepper.

Serve with plain boiled potatoes and spinach.

HADDOCK AU GRATIN

Pre-heat oven to 180°C/350°F or gas mark 4
To serve 3–4:

½ lb/250 g mushrooms
½ pint/30 cl milk
dash of cayenne pepper
1 teaspoon of salt
1 lb/500 g filleted haddock

1 oz/30 g butter
¼ pint/15 cl double cream
1 egg white
¼ lb/125 g grated Parmesan cheese

Peel and slice the mushrooms, boil in the milk with a little of the butter and add a pinch of salt and pepper. Boil for two or three minutes. Strain off the milk and reserve.

Rinse and skin the fish, remove bones and dry thoroughly. Place the fish in a buttered fireproof dish, pour the milk over it with a pinch of cayenne pepper, cover with greaseproof paper and poach for fifteen minutes in the oven at 180°C/350°F or gas mark 4. Mix the cream and the mushrooms and pour over the fish. Beat the egg white to a froth and spread over the fish fillets and sprinkle with cheese. Raise the oven temperature to 220°C/425°F or gas mark 7 and bake until light brown.

OVEN-BAKED HADDOCK

Pre-heat oven to 180°C/350°F or gas mark 4
To serve 6:

1 haddock, 2–3 lbs/1–1.5 Kg in weight	1 tablespoon tomato purée
1 teaspoon of salt	½ pint/30 cl creamy milk
fish farcie (for recipe see page 223)	6 ozs shrimps
flour	½ lb/250 g small button mushrooms
egg	1 tablespoon of grated Parmesan cheese
breadcrumbs	1 tablespoon of chopped fresh parsley, to garnish
2 ozs/60 g butter	

Clean the fish, keep the head but remove eyes and backbone. Rub the fish inside and out with salt and stuff with the fish farcie. Then close the fish and dip in flour, beaten egg and breadcrumbs. Place in a baking tin with melted butter, mixed with tomato purée. Bake in the oven at 180°C/350°F or gas mark 4 for ten minutes. Baste the fish with the butter, then add the milk and cook for fifteen minutes, basting with the sauce at intervals.

Add the mushrooms and shrimps and cook for a further ten minutes. Place the fish on a serving dish and garnish with the shrimps and the mushrooms. Add the Parmesan cheese to the sauce left in the pan, mix well and pour over the fish. Garnish with fresh parsley.

Serve with plain boiled new potatoes and peas.

BUCKLING AU GRATIN

Pre-heat oven to 220°C/425°F or gas mark 7
To serve 6:

3 tomatoes, skinned,
   de-seeded and cut in strips
½ onion, finely chopped and
   lightly fried in butter
6 buckling

1 oz/30 g butter
½ pint/30 cl creamy milk
1 oz/30 g grated Gruyère
   cheese

Buckling, a form of smoked herring, is a popular dish in Sweden, but not so well-known here. This is a way of cooking buckling that you are sure to enjoy.

Place the tomatoes with the fried onions in a gratin dish and put the buckling fillets on top. Dot over the butter, pour the milk and cheese on top, sprinkle with breadcrumbs and place in the oven set at 220°C/425°F or gas mark 7 to bake for ten to fifteen minutes until golden-brown.

BAKED HERRING IN TOMATO SAUCE

Pre-heat oven to 220°C/425°F or gas mark 7
To serve 6:

6 medium-sized herrings
1 teaspoon of salt
1 oz/30 g butter

1 teaspoon of anchovy essence
1 tablespoon of tomato sauce
2 tablespoons of breadcrumbs

Clean and bone the herrings, sprinkle with salt inside and out and leave them for five minutes. Melt the butter and stir in the anchovy essence and tomato sauce.

Butter a 2-inch/50 mm deep fireproof dish, roll the herrings, place in the dish and sprinkle with breadcrumbs. Cover with the tomato sauce mixture and place in the oven at 220°C/425°F or gas mark 7 to bake for ten minutes until golden-brown.

Sprats are delicious prepared in the same way, but bake for five to six minutes only.

STUFFED MACKEREL

Pre-heat oven to 180°C/350°F or gas mark 4
To serve 4:

4 mackerel
½ a lemon
salt and pepper
½ lb/250 g breadcrumbs
2 tablespoons of cold butter

1 egg, beaten
2 tablespoons of chopped fresh
    parsley
2 tablespoons of melted butter

Rinse fish and leave the heads on. Slit and remove back-bones. Rub with lemon, salt and pepper. Mix the breadcrumbs, cold butter, egg and half the parsley to a paste and stuff the fish. Roll the mackerel in flour and then dip in the melted butter. Bake in the oven at 180°C/350°F or gas mark 4 for twenty minutes, basting once or twice with the butter.

Serve, glazed with butter and sprinkled with the remaining chopped parsley.

SOUSED MACKEREL

Pre-heat oven to 180°C/350°F or gas mark 4
To serve 4–6:

1 mackerel per person

For the marinade:
½ pint/30 cl water
¼ pint/15 cl vinegar
6 white peppercorns, crushed
½ onion, sliced

2 sprigs of dill
½ teaspoon of salt
sugar to taste

Mix all the ingredients for the marinade together in a saucepan and boil. Put the fish in a fireproof dish and pour over the marinade. Place in the oven at 180°C/350°F or gas mark 4 and cook for fifteen minutes. Remove, allow to cool and eat cold with horseradish sauce in mayonnaise, and creamed potatoes.

MACKEREL MARNIES

Pre-heat oven to 220°C/425°F or gas mark 7
To serve 4:

4 medium-sized mackerels
¼ pint/15 cl dry white wine
¼ pint/15 cl water
2 tablespoons of vinegar
1 bay leaf

10 black peppercorns
½ teaspoon of mustard-seed
1 large onion, sliced
1 tablespoon of dried red
   chillies, crushed

For the garnish:
lettuce
hard-boiled eggs

1 sprig of parsley
1 sprig of dill

Place the mackerel in a fireproof dish. Put all the other ingredients in a saucepan and bring to the boil. Pour over the mackerel, cover with greaseproof paper and place in the oven at 220°C/425°F or gas mark 7, to cook for fifteen to twenty minutes.

Allow to cool in the stock, then remove the mackerel and place on a bed of lettuce. The stock should settle into a jelly. Glaze the fish with the jellied stock and garnish with sliced, hard-boiled eggs, parsley and dill.

Serve with vinaigrette salad sauce (for recipe see page 216) and boiled potatoes. This dish can also be made with herring instead of mackerel.

SCOTCH KIPPERS

It gives me much pleasure to include the humble kipper in this chapter, which I consider to be a very special fish. If you buy the best quality kipper and cook it properly, it makes the most delicious dish.

This is the only way to cook a kipper.

First, you must use real Scotch kippers, properly cured, not, horror of horrors, *painted*. Cut off the head and tail of the kippers. Place them in a fireproof dish and rinse in boiling water. Leave about a tablespoon of hot water in the dish. Place a knob of butter on each kipper. Leave them under a hot grill for about four or five minutes, basting once or twice. When cooked, transfer to a serving plate and glaze with the melted butter.

Perform the whole operation as fast as you can and enjoy the benefits of one of the few really special dishes that require the minimum of preparation.

PRAWN COCKTAIL WITH EGGS

To serve 2:

2 eggs
2 anchovy fillets
¼ pint/15 cl mayonnaise mixed with 2 tablespoons of whipped cream
1 teaspoon of chopped chives
1 tablespoon of tomato sauce

dash of cayenne pepper
1 lettuce
4 ozs/125 g prawns, fresh or frozen
1 tablespoon of chopped radishes

Boil the eggs for six minutes (but do not hard-boil them), then shell in cold water. Chop the anchovies and blend with half the amount of mayonnaise mixture, add the chives, tomato sauce and cayenne pepper. Rinse and dry the lettuce thoroughly, cut in strips and put in the bottom of two glasses. Stand the eggs up in the middle, arrange the prawns around them and pour over the sauce. Cover with the rest of the mayonnaise mixture and decorate with chopped radishes.
Serve with melba toast.

SPICY PRAWN COCKTAIL

To serve 6:

2 lettuce hearts
¾ lb/350 g peeled prawns
4 tablespoons of mayonnaise
1 tablespoon of tomato sauce
1 teaspoon of brandy
dash of cayenne pepper

½ cucumber, thinly cut into strips
2 tablespoons of double cream
1 teaspoon of lemon juice
1 tablespoon of oil
salt, pepper and sugar to taste

This is a piquant prawn cocktail with a certain kick to it.
Rinse, dry, and cut lettuce into strips. Put a bed of lettuce in each

individual glass, mix the rest of the ingredients together and pile into the glasses.

PRAWNS AU GRATIN

To serve 4 as a first course:

1½ ozs/40 g butter	½ pint/30 cl creamy milk
1 oz/30 g plain flour	(heated)
1 teaspoon of curry powder	1 lb/500 g prawns
salt	1 tablespoon of brandy or
dash of cayenne pepper	sherry
2 tablespoons of tomato purée	1 oz/30 g grated cheese

Melt 1 oz/30 g of butter and add the flour, curry powder, seasoning and tomato purée. Stir and add the heated milk a little at a time. Stir until smooth, then simmer for ten minutes. Add the prawns and brandy or sherry. Bring to the boil and add the remaining butter. Dish up in a fire-proof dish, sprinkle with cheese and brown under the grill.

PRAWNS PIQUANT

To serve 6:

½ pint/30 cl white sauce	pinch of cayenne pepper
½ glass of sherry or white wine	pinch of sugar
1 tablespoon of tomato sauce	1½ lb/750 g peeled Dublin Bay
1 tablespoon of mayonnaise	prawns
½ teaspoon of salt	parsley, to garnish

To the white sauce add the sherry, tomato sauce, mayonnaise, salt, cayenne pepper and sugar. Blend well and simmer for two or three minutes. Pour over the prawns and garnish with parsley.

CASSOULET DE CREVETTES

To serve 6:

1½ ozs/40 g butter
1 oz/30 g plain flour
½ pint/30 cl fish stock (for recipe see page 221)
1 teaspoon of salt

pinch of cayenne pepper
2 tablespoons of double cream
2 tablespoons of dry white wine

You can serve this dish either as the fish course of a dinner party menu or as the main course of a light luncheon. It is the pinch of cayenne pepper that gives the extra kick to these delicious little fishes.

Make the sauce by melting the butter and then adding the flour. Once the flour is absorbed pour in the fish stock and seasoning and mix over a low heat. Add cream, and stir until the mixture thickens. Stir in the wine and then pour the sauce over the shrimps.

Serve in a pretty dish with melba toast.

SHRIMPS WITH RICE

To serve 2:

¼ lb/125 g rice
2 ozs/60 g butter
2 tablespoons of plain flour
1 large tin of asparagus tips
¼ pint/15 cl creamy milk
pepper, salt and sugar to taste

pinch of nutmeg
10 ozs/300 g shrimps
1 oz/30 g grated Gruyère cheese
1 sweet red or green pepper, finely sliced

Melt the butter, add the flour and mix in the juice from the tin of asparagus tips. Stir until smooth, then simmer for five or six minutes. Add the milk and seasoning, the nutmeg and the shrimps, leaving aside a few for decoration. Simmer for five minutes.

Meanwhile, boil the rice in salted water for ten to twelve minutes and place in a border round the serving dish. Scoop the shrimp mixture into the centre. Decorate the rice with the remainder of the shrimps and the asparagus tips. Sprinkle with the grated Gruyère cheese and pepper strips.

SCAMPI

To serve 4:

Dublin Bay prawns (4–6 per person)	6 ozs/175 g breadcrumbs
2 eggs, beaten	1 pint/60 cl cooking oil
	chopped fresh parsley

Dip the prawns in the beaten egg and then in the breadcrumbs. Deep-fry in boiling oil until golden. Drain and place in a napkin. Using a straining spoon, dip the parsley in the oil for a couple of seconds and then sprinkle over the scampi.

Serve with green tartare sauce (for recipe see page 215).

COQUILLES ST JACQUES BALMORAL

To serve 4:

4–6 scallops	1 tablespoon of butter
½ pint/30 cl milk	1 oz/30 g plain flour
6 peppercorns	1 oz/30 g grated Parmesan cheese
bay leaf	
salt and pepper	1 oz/30 g breadcrumbs

Remove the meat from the shells and cut it into pieces. Put in a saucepan with the milk, peppercorns and bay leaf, and season to taste. Bring to the boil and simmer for five minutes. Strain, but reserve the milk. Remove the peppercorns and bay leaf from the meat.

Put the butter into a saucepan, add the flour and strained milk. Simmer for five or six minutes, then add the cheese. Put half the sauce into the cleaned and buttered scallop shells and put the meat on top. Cover with the rest of the sauce, sprinkle breadcrumbs on top and brown under a hot grill.

OYSTERS IN WINE SAUCE

Pre-heat oven to 220°C/425°F or gas mark 7
To serve 4:

24 oysters
2 shallots, finely chopped
½ oz/15 g butter
4 or 5 mushrooms, peeled and sliced
½ tablespoon of chopped fresh parsley

2 tablespoons of breadcrumbs
½ glass of dry white wine
¼ pint/15 cl of double cream
2 tablespoons of grated Gruyère cheese
pepper and sugar, to taste

Remove the oysters from their shells and steam in their own juice for half a minute. Strain and save the juice for the sauce. Remove the beards and put the oysters in china scallop shells or small soufflé pots.

To make the sauce, fry the shallots in a little butter over a gentle heat, add the mushrooms, parsley, half the breadcrumbs and the wine. Stir and cook for one minute. Add the cream and the oyster juice. Remove from heat and add half the cheese. Season with pepper and a pinch of sugar. Cover the oysters with the mixture. Sprinkle the oysters with the remaining cheese and breadcrumbs, add a knob of butter and bake in the oven at 220°C/425°F or gas mark 7 for ten minutes until light brown.

ROULADES DE SAUMON FUMÉE

To serve 6–8:

½ pint/30 cl double cream
1 tablespoon of grated horseradish
juice of ½ a lemon
½ lb/250 g prawns, fresh or frozen

½ lb/250 g smoked salmon, thinly sliced
French lettuce
lemon slices, to garnish

There cannot be a more luxurious first course than this for an affluent dinner party.

Whip the cream, add the horseradish and lemon juice. Peel and rinse the fresh prawns in salted water or defrost frozen prawns. Add the prawns to the cream, put a spoonful of the mixture on the slices of smoked salmon and roll up lightly. Serve on a bed of French lettuce. Garnish with twisted slices of lemon, and serve with brown bread and butter, thinly sliced.

BALMORAL SALMON

One of the pleasantest interludes when I worked for the Royal Family was a stay at Balmoral while the Queen Mother was there with Prince Charles and Princess Anne, who were then still children. This was virtually in the nature of a holiday for me as the Buckingham Palace staff were there, and such was the below stairs protocol that I would not have dared bake so much as a cake without a formal request from the chef.

Towards the end of July there was always a great upheaval in royal households. Preparations for the annual holiday at Balmoral would start a week or so beforehand. Pots, pans, china and utensils, everything in fact except the Buckingham Palace stove, would be packed up and sent ahead. On the appointed day the staff of Buckingham Palace and Clarence House met on the station at Kings Cross and waited for a special train to take them to Ballater.

On my first journey I remember being amazed that even Buckingham Palace could hold so many people, until I realised that many were taking their wives, children and domestic animals as well. The scene reminded me of a king from ancient history moving camp.

Whenever the Queen went to Balmoral, Windsor or Sandringham, her chief chef, his four principal assistants and a staff that varied from fifty to two hundred, according to the length of the stay, would go with her. The remaining staff at Buckingham Palace would then go on a system known as board wages. Board wages is an old-fashioned system whereby the staff can either eat in the palace or take the money to buy their own food. At the palace there were six male chefs and a staff of about five hundred, all of whom had to be fed. It would have been

Salmon trout farcie in aspic (p. 51)

impossible to keep all the royal palaces fully staffed, so every now and again there was this great move.

At Balmoral all the Royal Family would lead an outdoor life, but of the ladies, it was the Queen Mother who was the most energetic. Her great passion was for salmon fishing, and this she did with intense concentration for hours on end. She would put on waders and old clothes and attempt to catch the biggest salmon she could find. She liked no interruption and took with her only the simplest of cold picnics.

Once, after two whole days of concentrated fishing, the Queen Mother presented me with two salmon, one of which must have weighed about 20 lbs. "Do what you like with them," she said. "Why not give the staff a treat?"

As there was only one rather small, and very old-fashioned refrigerator at Balmoral, I sent the large salmon to Clarence House to be put in the deep freeze to await my return, and cooked the smaller one according to this recipe.

To serve 4–6:

1 salmon	2 teaspoons of salt
1 carrot, sliced	1 dessertspoon of vinegar
1 small onion, sliced	parsley, chopped
10 white peppercorns	

For the lemon sauce:

$\frac{1}{2}$ pint/30 cl double cream	pinch of sugar
$\frac{3}{4}$ pint/40 cl mayonnaise	juice of $\frac{1}{2}$ lemon
$\frac{1}{2}$ teaspoon of mustard paste	

Rinse salmon and drain and place in a large saucepan with the sliced carrot, onion, peppercorns, salt and vinegar. Just cover with water and bring to the boil. Reduce heat and keep hot for five minutes. When dishing up, remove skin and bone without breaking the flesh and drain well.

To make the sauce, whip cream, stir in mayonnaise, gradually add mustard, sugar and lemon juice. Serve cold with the salmon garnished with the chopped parsley and accompanied by small boiled potatoes and cucumber salad.

Lobster in aspic (p. 53)

SAUMON COURT BOUILLON

To serve 4:

4 slices of salmon	bunch of parsley
pinch of sugar, salt and pepper	1 carrot
10 white peppercorns	1 large onion

Rinse the salmon slices and place in a flat, shallow pan. Add water to cover, seasoning, peppercorns, parsley and sliced vegetables. Cover with greaseproof paper. Place pan over heat and bring to the boil. Lower the heat and simmer for five or six minutes. Remove and keep hot. Remove skin and bones without breaking the fish.

Place on a serving dish and cover with some hollandaise sauce (for recipe see page 213). Serve the rest of the sauce separately.

Serve boiled new potatoes with butter and dill.

TRUITE EN BLEU ROYALE

To serve 6:

6 blue trout weighing	1 oz/30 g plain flour
6 ozs/175 g each	salt and pepper
½ lb/250 g butter	

For the tarragon sauce:

½ lb/250 g butter	1 tablespoon of dry tarragon
½ tablespoon of tarragon	leaves
vinegar	pinch each of salt, pepper,
juice of ½ lemon	cayenne and sugar

This is a dish of the utmost simplicity, but one which repays careful attention to detail. The boning of the fish is easily done if a nice, clean slit is made in the stomach and the backbone removed from the tail end.

The flesh of the blue trout should be a firm whitish pink. Remove scales, fins and the backbone but not the head. Remove as many small bones as possible. Rinse well and drain on a towel for ten minutes. Open and season, then close. Melt butter in frying pan. Dip the trout in the flour and cook gently in the butter until golden-brown, about five minutes each side. When cooked, place in a dish with a little butter and cover with greaseproof paper before serving.

To make the tarragon sauce, cream the butter in a basin and gradually work in the vinegar and lemon juice. Stirring all the time, add the tarragon leaves, salt, pepper, cayenne and small pinch of sugar. The texture should be light and creamy.

This dish is delicious with cucumber salad and piped creamed potatoes.

SALMON TROUT FARCIE IN ASPIC

Pre-heat oven to 170°C/325°F or gas mark 3
To serve 4–6:

1 salmon trout, about 2½ lbs/1 Kg

For the stuffing:
½ lb/250 g lemon sole, filleted
2 ozs/60 g butter
½ lb/250 g prawns
¼ pint/15 cl creamy milk

1 oz/30 g plain flour
2 eggs, separated
pepper, salt and sugar to taste

For the poaching liquid:
juice from a tin of asparagus tips
¼ pint/15 cl dry white wine

parsley
4 slices of onion
6 white peppercorns

For the garnish:
prawns
rings of green pepper
hard-boiled eggs

tomato purée
asparagus tips

For the aspic:
½ oz/15 g gelatine

1 pint/60 cl clear fish stock
(for recipe see page 221)

This is a party dish which always looks immensely graceful and is as good to eat. To me it epitomises the British table at its best. How I would love to do it again for a summer dance, perhaps, with the guests in gauzy dresses drifting around as they do in a Jean Anouilh play, or as cool refreshment after an elegant race meeting. It is a dish to bring out a sense of occasion.

Get your fishmonger to remove the backbone and gills of the fish but leave the head intact. When you get it home wash and dry the fish and sprinkle some salt inside.

Make the stuffing by scraping the fillets of lemon sole from the skin, making sure there are no bones, then putting through the mincer with the butter and prawns. Mince three times and put in a basin. In another basin make a liquid mixture of the milk, flour, two egg yolks, pepper, salt and sugar to taste. Mix really smooth and then gradually add it a little at a time to the fish cream, stirring continuously. Whip egg whites to a stiff froth and fold into the fish cream.

Place the salmon trout in a flat pan and stuff it with the fish cream. Pour into the pan the asparagus juice and the wine. Add the parsley, onion rings and peppercorns. Cover with greaseproof paper before putting on the lid. Heat to just below boiling point, then transfer to the oven which has been pre-heated to 170°C/325°F or gas mark 3, to poach for twenty minutes. When cooked, remove covering and let it cool. When cold, remove skin very gently so as not to break the flesh. Place the fish carefully on a dish and garnish with prawns down the centre, alternating with green pepper rings.

To make the aspic, dissolve the gelatine in a little water and add to the heated fish stock. When mixed let the aspic cool until it is nearly, but not quite, set. Then spoon the aspic over the fish until it is well covered.

Decorate round the dish with hard-boiled egg whites stuffed with the sieved yolks mixed with tomato purée. Place bunches of asparagus tips between the eggs.

Serve with a mild-flavoured mayonnaise and lettuce and cucumber salad.

LOBSTER IN ASPIC

To serve 8–10:

2 cooked lobsters, about 1¾ lbs/850 g each
1 pint/60 cl fish aspic (see previous recipe), coloured green

2 hard-boiled eggs
1 sweet red pepper

For the stuffed tomatoes:
½ pint/30 cl mayonnaise
2 tablespoons of chopped fresh parsley
¼ pint/15 cl double cream

6 tomatoes
salt and pepper
2 hard-boiled eggs

For the garnish:
lettuce
cucumber

lemon slices

Like the previous recipe (salmon trout farcie in aspic), this is a dish that always looks elegant and is suitable for any special occasion.

Cut the lobsters in half lengthwise, break the claws gently and remove the meat from claws and tail. Remove all shell and bones, but retain the creamy green portion for the stuffed tomatoes.

Make the aspic according to the previous recipe and colour it green. This is done by blanching, then draining 1 lb/500 g of spinach and squeezing it through muslin to obtain a green liquid which is then added to the aspic. Alternatively, you can add 1 or 2 drops of green vegetable dye, bought in bottles. Fill the bottom of a mould with the green aspic, and leave it to cool. Decorate the mould with slices of hard-boiled egg and the red pepper cut in strips. Sprinkle a little aspic on top to keep the decorations in place.

Cut the lobster meat into neat pieces and place the best of them down the sides and the bottom of the mould. Then fill the mould up with the cooled but still liquid, aspic. Place in a refrigerator to set for two hours. When solid, loosen the aspic round the edges of the mould carefully with a knife, then dip the mould quickly in hot water. Place a cold dish on top of the mould and turn quickly upside down. Decorate the dish with cubes of cut aspic.

To make the stuffed tomatoes, sieve the soft creamy part of the lobster and mix this with a little warm aspic. Let it cool and, when nearly set, stir in some seasoned mayonnaise mixed with parsley and a little cream. Skin and cut the tomatoes in half, remove seeds, season and pipe in the lobster cream. Top with the sieved hard-boiled egg yolks and place the tomatoes round the lobster.

Serve with lettuce and cucumber garnished with lemon twists.

LOBSTER THERMIDOR

Pre-heat oven to 220°C/425°F or gas mark 7
To serve 2:

1 large cooked lobster	1 tablespoon of tomato purée
1 oz/30 g butter	3 fl oz/8 cl double cream
2 tablespoons of plain flour	1 tablespoon of brandy
½ pint/30 cl milk, heated	1 oz/30 g grated Gruyère
salt and sugar	cheese
pinch of cayenne pepper	watercress, to garnish
dash of Tabasco sauce	

Cut lobster in half lengthways, remove claws and tail, crack the claws and remove the meat. Cut the meat into pieces.

Melt the butter and flour and add the heated milk. Mix until smooth and thick, season and add tomato purée. Simmer for five minutes. Stir in the cream and add the lobster meat and brandy. Keep hot. Trim the lobster shell, leaving the legs and fill with the thermidor mixture. Sprinkle cheese on top and place in the oven at 220°C/425°F or gas mark 7 for ten minutes to brown.

Dish up on watercress.

FRIED OYSTERS

To serve 2:

1 dozen oysters	lemon quarters and parsley, to
1 tablespoon of double cream	garnish
plain flour	

This makes for a really first-class hors d'oeuvre.

Remove the oysters from their shells and steam for half a minute in their own juice. Put them in a basin with the juice. Add the cream and leave to stand for ten minutes. Remove from the liquid and roll in flour, then fry in hot oil until golden-brown. Garnish with lemon quarters and parsley.

CRAB VOL-AU-VENT

To serve 4:

1 large puffed pastry case	2 tablespoons of plain flour
1 packet of frozen fish cream	3 fl ozs/8 cl white wine
¾ pint/40 cl creamy milk	2 ozs/60 g butter
salt, pepper and sugar to taste	¼ lb/125 g frozen prawns
1 tin of crab meat	watercress, to garnish

The following is an 'easy-way-out' dish in that almost all the ingredients are canned, frozen or ready-made. All you have to do is buy them and then mix them altogether – and very good it is, too.

Warm the vol-au-vent case and keep until required. Cook the fish cream in half the amount of milk. Add seasoning and steam over a gentle heat until set. Strain and cool. Cut the crab meat in bits. Add the flour to the strained milk and cook over a gentle heat, stir until thick and smooth. Add the rest of the milk and wine. Simmer for five or six minutes and lastly add the butter.

Put in the crab meat and the prawns, leaving some aside for garnishing, taste for flavour and bring to the boil over a gentle heat. Remove at once and fill the pastry case with the mixture.

This dish looks its best served on a silver plate, garnished with watercress and a few whole prawns.

STUFFED PANCAKES WITH CREAM OF FISH AND SHRIMPS

Pre-heat oven to 180°C/350°F or gas mark 4
To make 8 thin pancakes:

¼ lb/125 g plain flour
1 egg
1 egg yolk
pinch of salt

½ pint/30 cl milk
nut oil for frying
scant butter
parsley sprigs, to garnish

For the filling:
½ pint/30 cl fish cream
(for recipe see page 223)

½ lb/250 g peeled frozen
   shrimps, defrosted

Place the flour in a basin, break in the whole eggs and the egg yolk, mix together and add the salt. Add the milk little by little. Put enough nut oil in a small saucepan to coat the bottom and heat gently. When hot pour enough batter in to make a thin pancake. Fry on both sides.

Mix the fish cream with the shrimps and fill the pancakes with the mixture. Roll up and place on a well-buttered baking sheet, cover with buttered greaseproof paper and place in the oven set at 180°C/350°F or gas mark 4 for five minutes. Dish up and glaze the pancakes with a little butter.

Decorate with parsley and serve hot or cold.

CUTLETS OF HALIBUT GRATINÉE

To serve 4–6:

2 lbs/1 Kg middle cut of
   halibut
salt
2 eggs
2 tablespoons of milk

flour
breadcrumbs
3 ozs/90 g butter
½ a lemon

For the sauce:
4 tablespoons of mayonnaise   juice of ½ a lemon
¾ pint/40 cl double cream   1 teaspoon of diluted mustard

For the garnish:
4 slices of lemon   anchovy fillets
chopped capers

Cut the fish into one-inch thick cutlets, remove skin and bone, rinse and dry on a cloth and sprinkle with salt. Beat a couple of eggs with the milk. Turn the fish in flour, coat in the egg mixture and then breadcrumbs. Melt the butter in a frying pan over a gentle heat and fry the fish cutlets golden-brown on both sides for ten to fifteen minutes. Make sure the fish is well cooked in the middle. Squeeze lemon juice over the cutlets.

For the sauce, mix the mayonnaise, cream, lemon and mustard together and serve separately.

Garnish the cutlets with the lemon slices, the anchovies in rings on top, and the chopped capers in the middle.

CUTLETS OF PLAICE IN BUTTER

To serve 2:

4 fillets of plaice   2 eggs, beaten
salt and pepper   lemon slices and fresh parsley,
plain flour   to garnish
2 ozs/60 g butter

This is a very simple but delicious dish. Skin, rinse and dry the fillets. Season with salt and pepper. Spread some flour on greaseproof paper. Fold the fillets in half so that the inside is on the outside, turn them in the flour and dip in the beaten egg. Put the butter in a frying pan and place over a low heat. Heat gradually but do not let the butter turn brown. Drop the fish in the hot butter and fry about three minutes on each side until golden-brown.

Dish up and garnish with lemon slices and fresh parsley. Serve with peas or spinach.

FILET DE SOLE MEUNIÈRE

To serve 6:

6 fillets of Dover sole
3 ozs/90 g butter
2 tablespoons of plain flour

1 teaspoon of salt
chopped parsley and lemon
  slices, to garnish

Rinse and skin the fillets of sole, place on a cloth to dry. Toss the fillets in seasoned flour and then dip in the butter which has been melted in a frying pan. Place in a fireproof dish and grill to a golden colour.

Dish up and sprinkle a line of finely chopped parsley on top. Garnish with slices of lemon.

SOLE À LA SAUCE RÉMOULADE

Pre-heat oven to 180°C/350°F or gas mark 4
To serve 4:

2 filleted Dover soles
seasoning
½ pint/30 cl good fish stock (for
  recipe see page 221)

1 lb/500 g of potatoes, mashed
  and creamed
½ pint/30 cl shrimps
parsley

For the rémoulade sauce:
4 hard-boiled eggs
3 egg yolks
¼ pint/15 cl olive oil
¼ pint/15 cl tarragon vinegar

1 tablespoon of French or
  English mustard paste
1 tablespoon of capers
4 anchovies
½ pint/30 cl whipped cream

Rinse fillets and dry well. Season and place in a tin with the stock. Cover with greaseproof paper and poach in the oven, set at 180°C/350°F or gas mark 4 for fifteen minutes.

To make the sauce, put the yolks of the hard-boiled eggs through a sieve, stir in the raw yolks and mix to a smooth paste. Add the oil and vinegar gradually, mixing all the time, then the mustard, capers and anchovies. Lastly, stir in the whipped cream.

Border a dish with the creamed potatoes, drain the fish and arrange in the middle. Coat with the rémoulade sauce and decorate with shrimps and parsley.

FILLET OF DOVER SOLE REGINA

Pre-heat oven to 220°C/425°F or gas mark 7
To serve 6:

1 lb/500 g lemon sole fillets	¼ pint/15 cl milk
½ bottle of champagne or dry white wine	3 eggs, separated
	2 cooked lobster, about
6 ozs/175 g butter	1½ lb/750 g each
½ pint/30 cl double cream	parsley, to garnish

For the sauce:

1 oz/30 g plain flour	1 pint/60 cl fish stock
3 ozs/90 g butter	(for recipe see page 221)

Skin and fillet the Dover soles. Cover some of the bones and heads with half the wine and ½ pint/30 cl water, bring to the boil and simmer for half an hour. Make a forcemeat with the lemon sole and 3 ozs/90 g of the butter by passing through the mincer three times. In another bowl mix the cream, milk and three egg yolks and stir into the forcemeat. Dissect the lobsters and add any small bits and pieces of lobster to the fish cream.

Rinse and dry the filleted Dover soles and season well. Keeping the underside on the inside, roll and stuff the fillets with the forcemeat. Place in a buttered fireproof dish with the rest of the wine and cover with greaseproof paper. Poach in the oven at 220°C/425°F or gas mark 7 for twenty minutes.

Remove the fillets and drain. Reduce the liquid by simmering. Make a sauce with the flour, 1 oz/30 g of butter, and the fish stock. Cook until it thickens. Lower heat and while simmering add the reduced liquid from the fillets. Remove from heat and strain the sauce. Stir in the remaining butter. Put the dissected lobster on top of each fillet and place on a serving dish. Coat with the sauce.

Garnish the border of the serving dish with the meat from the lobster claws and some parsley. Serve with button mushrooms steamed in butter, and new potatoes.

SOLE VALEOSKA

To serve 4–6:

For the sauce:

1 cooked lobster, about
  1¾ lbs/850 g in weight
½ pint/30 cl béchamel sauce (for
  recipe, see page 211)
1 tablespoon of tomato purée

salt and sugar
dash of cayenne pepper
¼ pint/15 cl sherry
¼ pint/15 cl double cream

For the sole:

2 lbs/1 Kg fillet Dover sole
salt
juice of 1 lemon
beaten egg

flour
breadcrumbs
parsley and lemon slices, to
  garnish

To make the sauce, cut the lobster in half lengthways, remove meat and cut into fairly large pieces, not forgetting the meat from the claws. Put the béchamel sauce in a pan, add the tomato purée, a pinch of sugar, salt, cayenne pepper and the sherry. Bring to the boil, reduce heat, add the lobster meat, and then stir in the cream. Simmer for five to ten minutes.

Cut the fillets of sole in half lengthways, and sprinkle with salt and lemon. Dip in flour, beaten egg and then coat in breadcrumbs. Twist the fillets and fry in deep oil. Drain on absorbent paper.

Pour the sauce onto a serving dish and pile the sole in the middle. Garnish with parsley and slices of lemon.

RED MULLET POACHED IN WINE

Pre-heat oven to 220°C/°425°F or gas mark 7
To serve 2:

2 red mullet weighing about
  ¾ lb/350 g each
lemon
salt
2 ozs/60 g butter

plain flour
pepper
¼ pint/15 cl dry white wine
pinch of cinnamon

Lobster thermidor (p. 54)
OVERLEAF, LEFT: *Fillet of Dover sole Regina (p. 59)*
OVERLEAF, RIGHT: *Turbot Café de Paris (p. 62)*

It was the Queen Mother, who has a very wide knowledge of fish, who introduced me to red mullet. I am grateful to her for the introduction, as it is really a very lovely fish. This is the way I cooked it for her at Birkhall.

Leave on the heads of the red mullet. Rinse and rub the fish inside with lemon and salt. Melt the butter in a fireproof dish and dip the fish first in butter, then in flour and again in butter. Pour half the amount of wine over the mullet and sprinkle them with a very little cinnamon. Place in the oven set at 220°C/425°F or gas mark 7. After five minutes, add the rest of the wine and then poach for a further ten minutes.

Serve plain.

POACHED TURBOT IN BUTTER SAUCE

Pre-heat oven to 170°C/325°F or gas mark 3
To serve 4:

4 fillets of turbot	1 tablespoon of plain flour
1 glass of dry white wine	juice of ½ a lemon
1 glass of fish stock (for	salt and pepper
recipe see page 221)	chopped parsley to garnish
2 ozs/60 g butter	

The day the King of Sweden, the late King Gustav VI, came to lunch was the only time I paid more attention to the tastes of the guest than of the host. I knew, though of course I had not been officially informed, that the King had a delicate stomach, so I planned accordingly. The dishes would have to be mild and bland but of the very best quality.

Afterwards, the King of my country asked to see me upstairs and said some very wonderful things about my cooking. It was a proud and happy day. It was this dish he liked particularly.

Poach the fillets in wine and stock in the oven set at 170°C/325°F or gas mark 3, for fifteen minutes. Dish up the fish and keep warm.

Melt 1 oz/30 g of the butter and add the flour. Mix well then strain the juice from the poached fillets into the pan. Stir over the heat and simmer gently for ten minutes. Mix in the lemon juice and stir in the remaining butter. Season with salt and pepper.

Glaze the fish with the sauce and garnish with parsley.

Entrecôte grill à la Bolognese (p. 68)

TURBOT CAFÉ DE PARIS

To serve 6:

2 lbs/1 Kg middle-cut of turbot
1 pint/60 cl fish stock, heated (for recipe see page 221)
¼ pint/15 cl dry white wine
juice of ½ a lemon
2 sprigs of parsley
salt and pepper

½ pint/30 cl mornay sauce (for recipe see page 212)
4 ozs/125 g frozen prawns, defrosted
grated Parmesan cheese
watercress and twists of lemon, to garnish

Cut the turbot into one-inch thick slices. Put them flat in the bottom of a shallow saucepan. Cover with hot fish stock and add the wine, lemon juice and the parsley. Season to taste. Cover the saucepan and bring to the boil. Lower the heat and just simmer for five or six minutes.

When the fish is cooked, remove from the stock, take off the skin and bones, being careful not to break the fillets. Pour a little of the mornay sauce on to the serving dish and place the fish fillets on top. Put the prawns on top of the fillets and cover with the rest of the sauce. Sprinkle Parmesan cheese over the top, place under the grill or in a hot oven for a few minutes, to turn a golden colour.

Before serving, place a bunch of watercress in the middle of the dish and decorate with one or two lemon twists.

TURBOT WITH HORSERADISH SAUCE

To serve 4:

2 lbs/1 Kg of middle-cut of turbot
1 pint/60 cl of boiling water
1 dessertspoon of salt

8 peppercorns
1 tablespoon of plain flour
1½ ozs/40 g cold butter
½ a grated horseradish

Turbot is a good rich fish and served according to this recipe as a main course, would need only a clear soup beforehand and perhaps a savoury afterwards to make a fine dinner party menu.

Cut the turbot into cutlets about two inches thick without removing the bone. Place the cutlets in boiling water, and add seasoning. Cover with greaseproof paper and steam for ten to fifteen minutes. Strain the fish stock and thicken with the flour to form a thick sauce. Add more seasoning to taste and then simmer for five minutes. Remove from heat and whisk in the cold butter little by little. Keep hot. Carefully remove skin and bones from the fish and place the cutlets on a dish. Cover the fish with some of the sauce. Serve the rest separately with the grated horseradish stirred in.

Serve with plain boiled potatoes in a white napkin.

Meat

THE MOST IMPORTANT PART OF EVERY MEAL IS THE MAIN DISH, AND IF YOU decide to serve meat, there is no likelihood of your being stuck for choice. All you have to do is make four main subdivisions – beef, lamb, veal and pork – which gives you about fifty different cuts from which to choose. After that you must consider whether you want to roast, grill, fry, braise, stew, poach or boil the meat. Then, of course, there are a million other little tricks from marinading to mincing that will provide a distinctive touch or two, plus a wide variety of suitable sauces and garnishes.

The recipes in this chapter pay tribute to the excellent quality of British meat, and the treatment accorded it is designed to enhance rather than disguise its fine flavour. With this in mind, I have included some traditional recipes like boiled leg of mutton with caper sauce and glazed saddle of veal, popular dishes which combine the best in British meat and cooking. The other recipes will, I hope, provide ideas for those days when inspiration and the sight of so much raw meat in your butcher's shop do not seem to march hand in hand.

Despite the fact that the quality of meat in this country is usually excellent, be ever vigilant. Treat your butcher as an ally and bear the following in mind. Lamb and mutton must be light red, with the fat creamy-white; beef should not be too dark; pork should be pale pink with the fat shining white; veal should be very pale. Never accept veal that is blue and blistered or, even worse, a mottled red colour.

BOILED BRISKET OF BEEF

To serve 6–8:

3 lbs/1.5 Kg rolled and boned
  brisket of beef
4 pints/2 litres water
1 tablespoon of salt
10 white peppercorns
2 carrots

3 onions
1 stick of celery
1 leek
1 tablespoon of chopped fresh
  parsley

Place the beef in a saucepan with enough water to cover. Bring to the boil and remove any scum. Add the salt and peppercorns, then cover and cook over a low heat for two and a half hours. Add the cut vegetables and a sprig of parsley, bring to the boil and simmer for another hour.

When the meat is cooked, cut some slices and place on a serving dish. Arrange the vegetables round the beef and moisten with a little stock. Sprinkle with chopped parsley on top. Serve with creamed potatoes and horseradish sauce.

The remaining stock is excellent for soup.

SALT SILVERSIDE WITH SUET DUMPLINGS

To serve 6–8:

3 lbs/1.5 Kg salt silverside
4 pints/2 litres water
10 peppercorns
1 leek
1 swede

2 carrots
3 onions
1 tablespoon of chopped fresh
  parsley

For the suet dumplings:
1 lb/500 g plain flour
1 teaspoon of baking powder
¼ teaspoon of salt

4 ozs/125 g beef suet
¼–½ pint/8–15 cl water

Place the silverside in a saucepan of cold water and bring to the boil. Remove scum and simmer for two hours. Peel and chop the vegetables, add to the pan and bring to the boil. Cook on a low heat for one hour.

Meanwhile to make the dumplings, mix the ingredients together in a basin. Make into small balls and drop these into boiling stock in a separate saucepan and cover. Boil gently for ten to twelve minutes and serve immediately with the silverside, which should be sliced and arranged on a serving dish. Place the vegetables around the meat, moisten with stock and sprinkle some chopped parsley on top.

CHATEAUBRIAND À LA ROSENBAD

To serve 4:

3 ozs/90 g butter	4 slices Chateaubriand steak,
½ tablespoon of oil	about 12 ozs/350 g in weight
	and 1½ inches/4 cm thick

For the sauce:

1 tablespoon of brandy	1 oz/30 g butter
3 fl ozs/8 cl sherry	dash of Worcester sauce
¼ pint/15 cl beef gravy	4 truffles, sliced, and the juice
2 tablespoons of liver paté	from the tin

I served this dish to the late King Frederik of Denmark when he paid a State visit in 1951. He was such a charming man that everyone was anxious to see he enjoyed his visit in every possible way. I can remember Prince Philip coming into the kitchen before his visit and discussing the food. I always enjoyed Prince Philip's informal visits. He would look into the saucepans, ask questions and crack some very good jokes. In times of stress and kitchen crises, he was a real morale booster. I appreciated the informality of these visits because normally a royal visit to the kitchen was preceded by a warning from above which made us feel we were in for a sort of kit inspection. Prince Philip, however, would appear without warning and take us as we were.

First, put the butter and the oil in a frying pan. When hot and golden-brown add the steaks and fry on both sides, basting a little. Cook for four to five minutes (underdone) or seven to eight minutes (medium), basting when necessary. Remove from the pan, reserving the juices for the sauce, and keep hot.

To make the sauce, pour the brandy into a clean pan. Heat and set alight, then pour in the sherry to extinguish the flame. Add beef gravy and the gravy from the steaks and boil for a few minutes. Add the liver paté, the butter, Worcester sauce and the juice from the truffles. Season to taste. Stir well, bring to the boil and strain the sauce over the Chateaubriand.

Garnish each steak with a slice of truffle. Serve with crisp fried potatoes and salad.

ENTRECÔTE GRILL À LA BOLOGNESE

To serve 2:

2 sirloin, porterhouse or T-bone steaks	seasoning
1 tablespoon of oil	½ lb/250 g mushrooms
1 oz/30 g marrow from marrow bones, chopped	¼ pint/15 cl red wine
	¼ pint/15 cl beef stock
1 clove of garlic, put through a garlic press	1 tablespoon of chopped fresh parsley

Trim unwanted fat from the steaks, brush with the oil and place on a grilling pan. Extract marrow from marrow bones by cutting bones into half-inch sections, place in salted water and boil for two minutes. Then shake marrow out of bone. Allow to chill and firm up before chopping. Mix the marrow with the garlic and put on top of the steaks. Grill for ten or fifteen minutes and place on a serving dish. Season to taste and keep hot. Add butter to the pan and toss the mushrooms. Arrange with the steaks. Add the wine and stock to the pan and stir well. Reduce the sauce until thick and then strain over the steaks. Sprinkle with chopped parsley and serve with legume salad (for recipe see page 157).

FILET DE BOEUF WITH SAUCE PIQUANT

Pre-heat oven to 220°C/425°F or gas mark 7
To serve 6–8:

3 lb/1.5 Kg undercut fillet of beef
salt and pepper

garlic salt
¼ lb/125 g bacon fat

For the sauce:
½ pint/30 cl beef stock
1 tablespoon of tomato sauce
¼ pint/15 cl of sherry

½ tablespoon of Worcester sauce
2 anchovy fillets

Rub the fillet with salt and pepper and sprinkle over a little garlic salt. Tie the bacon fat round the beef and cook in the oven at 220°C/425°F or gas mark 7. When brown on the outside, lower the heat, baste and roast for a further forty-five minutes. Baste every fifteen minutes with the meat juices. When cooked, untie the bacon, remove the meat from the pan, cut in thin slices and place in the middle of the serving dish.

To make the piquant sauce, add all the ingredients to the pan juices. Boil for one or two minutes until thickened. Then strain and serve with the beef.

SWEDISH HAMBURGER STEAKS

To serve 6:

1 lb/500 g rump steak, minced
2 ozs/60 g butter
½ pint/30 cl beef stock

1 teaspoon of Worcester sauce
1 tablespoon of tomato purée
6 poached eggs, to garnish

Cut the meat into pieces and remove unwanted skin and fat. Put through the mincer twice. Roll meat into a firm loaf and divide into six portions. Flatten them to one inch thick and criss-cross with a knife on top. Heat the butter in a frying pan and when the butter has turned light brown, put in the steaks and fry for three or four minutes on each side, basting all the time. Regulate the heat to prevent burning. Place the hamburgers on a serving dish and keep hot. Add the stock to the pan together with the Worcester sauce, a knob of butter, tomato purée and seasoning. Boil and reduce until thickened. Pour over the hamburgers. Place a poached egg on top of each and serve.

FILET MIGNON ARENBURG

To serve 6:

2 lbs/1 Kg fillet beef (the undercut)
6 slices of bread and butter
2 ozs/60 g butter
1 tablespoon of nut oil
1 teaspoon of garlic salt
salt and pepper to taste

½ pint/30 cl clear consommé (for recipe see page 16)
1 glass of Madeira wine or sherry
½ pint/30 cl bearnaise sauce (for recipe see page 214)
watercress, to garnish

Cut six small round steaks about one inch thick. Fry six rounds of bread and butter. Fry the steaks in butter and oil for two minutes on both sides, basting all the time. Dish up on the bread croûtons. Sprinkle with salt, pepper and garlic salt. Whisk out the pan with the consommé, a knob of butter and the Madeira wine or sherry. Place over a high heat and reduce to a glaze. Pour over the steaks.

Just before serving, cover each steak with a tablespoon of bearnaise sauce and garnish with watercress.

ENTRECÔTE STEAK WITH WINE SAUCE

To serve 6:

2 ozs/60 g fat bacon
salt and pepper to taste
1 clove garlic
2 lbs/1 Kg fillet of entrecôte steak
¼ pint/15 cl Madeira wine

1 tablespoon of nut oil
2 ozs/60 g butter
1 pint/60 cl heated beef stock
1 tablespoon of plain flour
¼ lb/125 g braised button mushrooms, to garnish

First, bully your butcher to see that the meat is well hung. Cut the bacon into long strips the same length as the steaks, which should be about half an inch thick. Season the strips with salt and pepper and rub with the garlic clove. Leave in a cold place to harden for half an hour. Trim the steaks of fat, gristle and skin, and rub with a couple of tablespoons of the Madeira wine and a tablespoon of oil mixed together. Leave to soak for one or two hours, turning the steaks once.

Insert the bacon strips with a larding needle, or with a sharp skewer, along the grain of the steak. Rub with salt and pepper and tie up with string making the fillet into a nice neat shape. Put an ounce of butter (25 g) and half a tablespoon of oil in an iron saucepan. The pan should be just big enough for the steak. When the butter and oil have turned golden-brown over the heat, put in the meat and braise it all round, using two wooden spoons to turn.

When the steak is brown all over, add half the amount of hot stock and half the wine. Cover the saucepan and braise for two or three hours, turning the fillet every half hour. Add some more stock after one hour and the rest of the wine half an hour before the end of the cooking time. When cooked, remove the fillet to a hot dish. Cut the fillet into thin slices and glaze with some of the gravy.

Put a tablespoon of flour into the rest of the sauce and stir well until absorbed. Skim the fat. Add the rest of the beef stock and stir until smooth. Simmer for ten to fifteen minutes. Strain and season to taste. Garnish the entrecôte with braised button mushrooms.

COLLOPS OF BEEF

To serve 6:

2 tablespoons of plain flour	2 lbs/1 Kg braising steak, cut in
$\frac{1}{4}$ teaspoon of pepper	slices
$\frac{1}{2}$ tablespoon of salt	6 peppercorns
2 ozs/60 g butter	1 bay leaf
$\frac{1}{2}$ tablespoon of corn oil	1 teaspoon of gravy browning
2 or 3 onions, chopped	

Mix the flour with the pepper and salt. Pound the steaks on both sides and dip them in the seasoned flour. Heat the saucepan (preferably an iron one) and put in the butter and oil. Add the chopped onion and braise a little. Add the meat and turn in the saucepan with a spoon. Put in the peppercorns and the bay leaf. Mix the gravy browning with a little hot water and add. Turn the meat once, add the water and bring to the boil on a high heat, then cover the saucepan and simmer for two or three hours.

When cooked, serve in a casserole or deep dish. Skim fat from gravy and add more hot water if it is too thick. Heat and pour the sauce over the meat.

Serve with plain boiled potatoes.

MARINADED BEEF ROULADES

Pre-heat oven to 170°C/325°F or gas mark 3
To serve 6:

2 lbs/1 Kg rump beef or
   topside

For the marinade:

$\frac{1}{2}$ tablespoon of oil $\frac{1}{2}$ teaspoon of salt
1 tablespoon of red wine or   pinch of white pepper and
   wine vinegar   pinch of garlic salt

For the stuffing:

$\frac{1}{2}$ lb/250 g minced smoked   1 tablespoon of tomato purée
   gammon   1 oz/30 g chopped anchovy
1 small onion, finely chopped   fillets
1 tablespoon of chopped fresh   1 oz/30 g butter
   parsley

For the sauce:

2 ozs/60 g butter $\frac{3}{4}$ pint/40 cl of beef stock or
1 tablespoon of plain flour   water
                                                    $\frac{1}{4}$ pint/15 cl of red wine

Cut the meat into two–inch slices, then flatten by pounding. Spread flat on a dish. Mix the ingredients for the marinade and pour over the meat. Let it stand for one hour, turning the meat once.

Filet mignon Arenburg (p. 70)

Mix the minced smoked gammon, onion, parsley, tomato purée, anchovies and butter well together. Remove the beef slices from the marinade, and spread the stuffing on the middle of each slice. Roll them up and fasten with a wooden skewer or tie with fine string.

To make the sauce, heat 2 ozs/60 g butter in a frying pan and brown the roulades all round. When brown put in a saucepan or casserole dish. Add the flour to the butter in the frying pan, stir until browned, then add the hot stock or water and stir until smooth. Simmer for five minutes. Strain the sauce into another pan, add the wine and bring to the boil. Pour over the roulades, cover with a lid and cook in the oven at 170°C/325°F or gas mark 3 or on top of the stove on a gentle heat for about two hours.

Serve in the casserole accompanied by plain boiled rice or creamed potatoes. Or for a special occasion, serve in a flat dish with a border of rice or pipe the creamed potatoes round the roulades. Garnish the border with quartered tomatoes, skinned and seeded, and place a sprig of parsley on each side.

BEEF STEAK AND KIDNEY PUDDING

To serve 4:

suet pastry (for recipe see
  page 225)
1 lb/500 g stewing steak
6 ozs/175 g ox kidney
2 ozs/60 g chopped onions or a
  small clove of garlic,
  chopped

salt and pepper
1 tablespoon of plain flour
½ pint/30 cl water
1 glass of sherry

Grease a pudding basin and line with the suet pastry. Make enough to cover and overlap the rim of the basin. Cut the stewing steak and kidney into small pieces, and remove unwanted fat and skin. Put in a bowl, add the onion or garlic, pepper and salt, and the flour. Mix together and place in the suet-lined basin. Add the water and sherry. Cover with the pastry overlapping the rim of the basin. Cover with greaseproof paper and tie a napkin over the top. Put the basin in a steamer containing boiling water which reaches three-quarters of the way up the basin. Boil

Marinaded beef roulades (p. 72)

for six or seven hours, topping up the boiling water when necessary.

To serve, undo the wrappings and fold a clean white napkin round the basin.

VAMPIRE STEAK

To serve 4:

1 lb/500 g rump or sirloin steak   1 onion, finely chopped
4 yolks of eggs   1 beetroot, chopped
2 tablespoons of capers

Scrape the steak very finely with a grater (mincing is not quite good enough) and roll into one long loaf. Cut into four portions and flatten so that each steak is half an inch thick. Make a dent in the centre of each steak, into which you put an unbroken egg yolk. Chop the capers and sprinkle them round the yolks, then add the chopped onion and beetroot.

Serve with horseradish sauce and mayonnaise.

SAILOR BEEF

Pre-heat oven to 170°C/325°F or gas mark 3
To serve 4–6:

2 lbs/1 Kg rump steak   butter
1 oz/30 g plain flour mixed $\frac{3}{4}$ pint/45 cl stock
   with 1 teaspoon of salt $\frac{1}{2}$ teaspoon gravy browning
2 lbs/1 Kg potatoes $\frac{1}{4}$ pint/15 cl claret
2 large onions   salt
$\frac{1}{2}$ lb/250 g mushrooms

When Prince Philip returned from his spell of duty in Malta as a naval officer there was, of course, great rejoicing at Clarence House. All sailors seem to enjoy their food with extra zest, and the standard of cooking is higher in the navy than in the other services. Sailors know good food when they see it, and Prince Philip was no exception. I can remember how much I enjoyed cooking for him on his return and how, with the staff, I plotted and planned in the kitchen for our welcome-home dishes. This was one of them.

Cut the meat into individual steaks half an inch thick, then pound them well. Turn the steaks in seasoned flour. Peel and cut the potatoes and onions in thick slices. Peel and slice the mushrooms and fry in butter. Mix the stock with the gravy browning and claret. Grease a casserole dish with 1 oz/30 g of butter. Place the potatoes on the bottom of the dish, cover with a layer of onions and place the beef steaks and mushrooms on top. Finish with another layer of potatoes and sprinkle with salt and pepper. Dot on knobs of butter and pour over the mixed wine and stock. Cover with a lid and braise on top of the cooker or in the oven at 170°C/325°F or gas mark 3 for two and a half hours.

FILLET OF BEEF WITH MUSHROOMS AND YORKSHIRE PUDDING

Pre-heat oven to 220°C/425°F or gas mark 7
To serve 8:

3 lbs/1.5 Kg fillet of beef from the undercut	1 lb/500 g mushrooms
1 clove of garlic	½ pint/30 cl beef stock (heated)
2 tablespoons of nut oil	1 tablespoon of tomato purée
butter	dash of Worcester sauce

Batter for Yorkshire puddings:

4 ozs/125 g plain flour	3 fl ozs/8 cl creamy milk
pinch of salt	lard
2 eggs	

There is no better meat in the world, in my opinion, than the undercut of British beef, sitting pinkly on a dish and bathed in its own glorious juices. It is a privilege to cook such marvellous meat and, remember, no-one knows quite how to cook it like the British. This was the first dish I set about learning when I came to this country and often, when living abroad since, I have been called upon by desperate British expatriates to show their cooks the right way of cooking beef. Roast beef is only really properly understood in Britain.

This is how I served it on one occasion to Lord Cromer, then Governor of the Bank of England. A dish, I thought, as solid and traditional as the Bank itself with, perhaps, that little extra touch of distinction such as possessed only by British bankers.

Trim the fillets and remove all skin, gristle and fat. Crush the garlic and add to the oil. Sprinkle pepper on the beef and smear all over with the garlic oil. Allow to stand for one hour.

Remove the pieces of garlic and tie the fillet with fine string to keep a nice shape. Place it in a roasting tin with the oil and 1 oz/30 g butter, and put in the oven preheated to 220°C/425°F or gas mark 7. Baste after fifteen minutes and reduce the heat a little. Roast for thirty-five minutes, basting occasionally.

Meanwhile, make individual Yorkshire puddings. Sift the flour with the salt. Beat the eggs with the water and make a well in the centre of the flour. Pour in the eggs, mixing in the flour little by little. Add the milk and beat for four or five minutes. Allow to rest for half an hour. Add half a teaspoon of lard to individual moulds and warm the tins. Beat the batter once more and then fill each tin half full with the mixture. Bake for fifteen minutes at the top of the oven or until crispy.

Ten minutes before the meat and Yorkshire puddings have finished cooking, braise the mushrooms in butter and keep hot until you are ready to serve.

When the meat is cooked, remove from the oven and keep warm while making the gravy. Skim off the oil from the roasting tin, add the heated stock and stir. Boil over a high heat, add the tomato purée, Worcester sauce and 1 oz/30 g of butter, and season to taste. Reduce to a glazed sauce. Remove the string from the beef, slice thinly and put together again, then glaze with a little of the sauce.

Surround the meat with the braised mushrooms and Yorkshire pudding. Pour over a little of the glazed sauce. Serve with crisp roast potatoes and broccoli, or petits pois and a fresh salad.

PINK BEEF

Pre-heat oven to 220°C/425°F or gas mark 7
To serve 12–16:

4 lbs/2 Kg sirloin or undercut of beef
1 tablespoon of nut oil
½ teaspoon of garlic salt
½ oz/15 g gelatine
½ pint/30 cl of beef stock

20 pickling onions
1 tablespoon of tomato juice
dash of Worcester sauce
grated horseradish and shredded lettuce, to garnish

Smear the beef with oil and sprinkle over some garlic salt. Roast at 220°C/425°F or gas mark 4 for fifteen minutes to seal the juices; baste, lower heat and cook for one hour. Dish up the beef, add the gelatine to the warm stock and pour into the pan used for cooking the beef. Boil the liquid so that it is reduced to a glaze and coat the beef with the gravy.

Cover the onions with water and cook with the lid off until the water evaporates. Add the tomato juice and Worcester sauce and simmer slowly.

When the beef has cooled on the dish, cut into thin slices and stick together again. Arrange the glazed onions round the beef. Make horseradish ribbons by using the large holes on the grater and decorate the dish with shredded lettuce and horseradish strips.

Mutton is the meat from a sheep that is over a year old, and in this country is now a rarity. It has more flavour than lamb and is firmer in texture although it is not as tough. If you are unable to buy mutton you may substitute lamb for the following three dishes and reduce the cooking time slightly.

BOILED LEG OF MUTTON (OR LAMB) WITH CAPER SAUCE

To serve 6–8:

4 lbs/2 Kg leg of mutton (or lamb, but see note on page 77)	sprig of parsley
	10 peppercorns
	salt and pepper
2 carrots	
1 onion	

For the caper sauce:

2 ozs/60 g plain flour	2 tablespoons of roughly-chopped capers
½ pint/30 cl mutton (or lamb) stock	salt, pepper and sugar to taste
juice of a lemon	2 egg yolks
¼ pint/15 cl creamy milk	a little milk or water
	1 tablespoon of butter

Rinse the meat in scalding water, place it in a pan and cover with boiling water. Add the whole vegetables, parsley, peppercorns, salt and pepper. Bring to the boil and simmer slowly for one and a half hours. When cooked remove from the stock and place on a dish to keep hot.

To make the sauce, put the flour and stock together in a saucepan and whisk until smooth. Add the lemon juice. Place over a low heat and bring to the boil, whisking all the time until thick. Add the milk gradually and boil over a low heat for five minutes. Add the capers and the seasoning. Beat the egg yolks with a little milk or water and add to the sauce. Remove from heat and stir in the butter.

Serve with Brussels sprouts and creamed potatoes.

NAVARIN OF MUTTON (OR LAMB)

To serve 6:

2 lbs/1 Kg leg of mutton (or lamb, but see note on page 77)	2 lambs kidneys
	1 tablespoon of plain flour
	3 ozs/90 g butter
1 lb/500 g mushrooms	salt and pepper to taste
2 carrots	12 small onions

¼ pint/15 cl stock
3 fl ozs/8 cl red wine
1 teaspoon of sugar

1 tablespoon of chopped fresh
  parsley

Remove unnecessary fat from meat and cut the meat into two-inch squares. Cut the mushrooms in half, dice the carrots and cut the kidneys into slices. Sprinkle the meat with flour and braise in butter until light brown. Season to taste and place in a pan with the carrots. Braise the onions and mushrooms in butter quickly and add to the pan.

Pour the stock into the frying pan, heat and stir. Strain over the meat, add the wine and sugar and bring to the boil. Cover and cook on a low heat for one and a half hours. Stir once or twice during cooking.

Serve with sprinkled parsley on top.

RAGOÛT OF MUTTON (OR LAMB)

Pre-heat oven to 180°C/350°F or gas mark 4
To serve 6:

1 shoulder of mutton (or lamb,
  but see note on page 77)
  about 3 lbs/1.5 Kg
2 onions
2 carrots
2 pints/1.25 litres water
salt and pepper

small root of parsley
10 peppercorns
1 oz/30 g plain flour
2 eggs
4 oz/125 g breadcrumbs
2 ozs/60 g melted butter

Ask your butcher to chop the shoulder in ½ lb/250 g portions and remove the top skin. Trim off any unnecessary fat and put in a pan with the vegetables and water to cover. Bring to the boil and remove any scum. Add salt, pepper, parsley and peppercorns and boil for one hour. Remove the meat, allow to cool a little and dip portions into flour, beaten egg and then breadcrumbs. Place in a roasting tin, moisten with 2 ozs/60 g melted butter and cook in the oven at 180°C/350°F or gas mark 4 for one hour. Turn the meat once during cooking and baste with the fat.

When cooked the meat should be tender, crisp and brown on top.

Serve with creamed potatoes, Brussels sprouts and puréed onion sauce. The remaining stock will be an excellent basis for soup or sauces.

ROAST BREAST OF LAMB

To serve 4:

1 breast of lamb	1 small swede, halved
salt to taste	10 white peppercorns
2 onions, halved	

Place the breast of lamb in a saucepan and cover with hot water. Add salt, the halved onions, the halved swede and peppercorns. Bring to the boil and boil for twenty minutes. Remove from water, place in a roasting tin and grill for twenty-five minutes, basting every ten minutes. Or put on a spit and cook for half an hour.

Serve with boiled new potatoes and mint jelly.

LAMB CUTLETS

To serve 6:

12 fillets of lamb	4 ozs/125 g breadcrumbs
2 tablespoons of chopped fresh parsley	1 tablespoon of oil
	6 slices of bottled cucumber
2 ozs/60 g butter	redcurrant jelly
salt and pepper	1 tablespoon of mushroom
1 oz/30 g plain flour	sauce (for recipe see page 114)
2 eggs	½ pint/30 cl stock

Beat and flatten the fillets. Mix the chopped parsley and 1 oz/30 g of butter together and place a dollop on top of six of the steaks. Sprinkle with salt and pepper, then place the other six steaks on top like a sandwich.

Turn them carefully in flour, beaten egg and then breadcrumbs and fry in remaining butter and oil over a gentle heat for ten or fifteen minutes until golden-brown. Place on a serving dish.

Put the mushroom sauce in the frying pan, add the stock and boil to reduce a little. Strain over the cutlets. Place a slice of cucumber on top of each and serve with redcurrant jelly.

MINCED LAMB CUTLETS

To serve 4:

½ lb/250 g mushrooms
1 tablespoon of finely-
  chopped onion
1½ lbs/750 g lamb, minced
salt and pepper to taste

1 tablespoon of oil
¼ pint/15 cl stock
1 oz/30 g butter
dash of Worcester sauce

Mince the mushrooms and lightly fry the chopped onion in the oil. Mix together with the minced lamb and salt and pepper. Form into small cutlets about half an inch thick and fry in the oil on a gentle heat for six minutes on each side.

Swirl out the pan with the stock, add butter and a dash of Worcester sauce. Bring to the boil and strain over the cutlets.

SADDLE OF LAMB AU GRATIN

Pre-heat oven to 220°C/425°F or gas mark 7
To serve 8:

4 lbs/2 Kg saddle of spring
  lamb

1 teaspoon of salt
¼ teaspoon of white pepper

For the sauce:
½ lb/250 g mushrooms
1 onion
1½ ozs/40 g butter
1 tablespoon of plain flour
salt and pepper to taste
¼ pint/15 cl good beef or
  mutton gravy

1 tablespoon of Madeira wine
1 tablespoon of double cream
2 ozs/60 g grated Gruyère
  cheese
2 ozs/60 g toasted white
  breadcrumbs
1 tablespoon of oil

Wring out a cloth in hot water and wipe the saddle. Remove top skin and unwanted fat and trim . Season with salt and pepper. Tie the saddle at both ends with string to keep in shape. Roast in the oven at 220°C/425°F or gas mark 7 for 1¼ hours, basting frequently.

While the saddle is cooking make the gratin mixture. Peel the mushrooms and chop into small pieces, peel the onion and chop finely. Put the butter in a pan to brown and braise the mushrooms and onion lightly. Sprinkle over flour and cook for two minutes stirring all the time. Season to taste and add the hot gravy. Stir well and cook for five or six minutes. Reduce heat and add the Madeira wine, cream and half the cheese. Stir well, remove from heat and keep hot.

When the saddle is cooked, remove the string and slice the two fillets from the top. Remove the two small under fillets and cut them into one-inch thick slices diagonally. Spread the cheese and mushroom sauce on top of the meat. Sprinkle the remaining cheese over the top and cover with breadcrumbs mixed with butter. Moisten with the oil and place in the oven to brown for ten or fifteen minutes.

Dish up and garnish with spring peas and small potatoes braised in butter. Serve with plain salad and redcurrant jelly.

GIGOT D'AGNEAU AU FOUR

Pre-heat oven to 220°C/425°F or gas mark 7
To serve 4:

4 middle cuts of lamb steaks from the leg (about ½ lb/ 250 g each)	½ lb/250 g potatoes, peeled and sliced
salt and pepper	10 small onions
2 tablespoons of plain flour	½ pint/30 cl stock
3 ozs/90 g butter	1 tablespoon of tomato purée
2 carrots	1 tablespoon of chopped fresh parsley

Pound the steaks a little, sprinkle with pepper and salt and toss in flour. Melt 1 oz/30 g of the butter in a roasting tin. Put in the carrots (cut lengthways), the potatoes and the onions and brown over a low heat. Bring the hot stock mixed with the tomato purée to the boil and pour over the vegetables. Place in the oven pre-heated to 220°C/425°F or gas mark 7 and cook for half an hour.

Braise the meat in the remaining butter on both sides until brown and put with the vegetables in the roasting tin. Add the potatoes and bake in the oven for three-quarters of an hour, or until the meat is tender. Dish up and serve the meat on a bed of vegetables. Garnish with parsley.

HARICOT LAMB

To serve 4:

2 lbs/250 g best end of spring lamb
1 oz/30 g butter
1 tablespoon of plain flour
salt and pepper, to taste
½ lb/250 g mushrooms
½ clove of crushed garlic
½ pint/30 cl good stock
½ glass of sherry
1 tablespoon of redcurrant jelly
¼ pint/15 cl double cream
gravy browning (optional)

Ask the butcher to chine the backbone, remove the top skin and cut the best end of lamb into double cutlets. Trim the cutlets and brown in butter, sprinkle over with flour and braise. Season and add the mushrooms, peeled and cut into slices, the garlic, hot stock, sherry and the redcurrant jelly. Mix gently, cover the pan and cook for one hour and fifteen minutes. Stir once or twice very gently to prevent any sticking at the bottom of the pan.

When ready, remove the cutlets and place in a deep dish. Add the cream to the sauce and a little gravy browning if necessary. The sauce should be a creamy, golden colour. Pour the sauce over the cutlets and serve with haricot beans.

GRILLED LAMB CUTLETS WITH PARSLEY BUTTER AND PURÉE OF GREEN PEAS

To serve 6:

6 double lamb cutlets, one per person
salt and pepper
¼ lb/125 g butter
1 tablespoon of chopped fresh parsley
juice of half a lemon
dash of Worcester sauce
1½ lbs/750 g peas
1 tablespoon of double cream
½ lb/250 g rice
1 sweet green pepper

Grill lamb cutlets for four to five minutes on each side and season with salt and pepper when cooked. Keep at low temperature. Soften but don't melt the butter in a separate pan, mix in chopped parsley, lemon juice and Worcester sauce. Refrigerate this mixture for half an hour and, just before serving, slice and place on each lamb chop.

Cook the peas, and sieve. Add a knob of butter, a tablespoon of cream, some salt and mix together. Keep hot.

Boil the rice for twenty minutes. Chop the pepper finely and mix in with the rice.

MINCED LAMB CUTLETS WITH CURRANT SAUCE

To serve 4:

¼ lb/125 g rice	1 egg
8 fl oz/225 cl stock	salt, pepper and sugar, to taste
1 large onion, chopped	plain flour
1 lb/500 g meat from under-done roast lamb	butter or bacon fat for frying

For the sauce:

1 tablespoon of plain flour	¼ pint/15 cl red wine or 3 fl oz/
½ pint/30 cl good stock	8 cl vinegar
¼ lb/125 g currants, washed and cleaned	salt and pepper
	1 tablespoon of brown sugar
	½ tablespoon of butter

Boil the rice in the stock with the chopped onion for twenty-five minutes. Strain and cool. Mince the meat and add the rice, the egg, salt, pepper and a little sugar. Mix well. Make into rissoles, dip in flour and fry to a golden brown in the butter or bacon fat over a slow heat. Dish up and keep hot.

To make the sauce, mix flour and stock in a saucepan and bring to the boil over a low heat, stirring until smooth. Add the currants, wine or vinegar, salt, pepper and brown sugar. Simmer for fifteen minutes, then stir in the butter.

Serve with the minced lamb cutlets and vegetables in season.

Pink beef (p. 77)
OVERLEAF, LEFT: *Navarin of lamb (p. 78)*
OVERLEAF, RIGHT: *Grilled lamb cutlets with parsley butter and purée of green peas (p. 83)*

LAMB NOISETTES

To serve 4:

8 lamb noisettes	1 teaspoon of Bovril
salt and pepper	1 glass of Madeira wine
4 ozs/125 g butter	1½ lbs/750 g mushrooms
Worcester sauce	1 lb/500 g petits pois
½ pint/30 cl stock	watercress, to garnish
1 tablespoon of tomato purée	

Ask your butcher to prepare the noisettes by cutting out the fillets from a loin of lamb, and cutting the fillets into 1½ inch slices. The noisettes should have a ribbon of fat fastened round them with a wooden stick.

Season the noisettes with salt and pepper and place in a pan. Place 2 ozs/60 g of the butter on top and grill for five or six minutes on both sides, basting once or twice, so that they are browned on the outside and a light pink inside.

While the noisettes are grilling, braise the mushrooms in the remaining butter and cook the petit pois. When the noisettes are ready, sprinkle a little Worcester sauce over them and place in a dish to keep hot. Pour the heated stock in the grilling pan and add the tomato purée, Bovril, the Madeira and a knob of butter. Transfer the sauce into a pan and boil until thick and glacé. Strain the sauce over the noisettes and then dish up the petits pois on a large serving dish. Arrange the mushrooms and petits pois on one side with the watercress in between.

Serve with mint jelly.

IRISH STEW

To serve 6–8:

2 lbs/1 Kg best end of neck of lamb	1 lb/500 g potatoes
seasoning to taste	chopped fresh parsley, to garnish
4 onions, sliced	

Have the neck chopped in double cutlets and see that the top skin has

Lamb noisettes (p. 85)

been removed. Trim away any fat. Put the cutlets in a saucepan of water, bring to the boil for five minutes. Drain off the water, clean out the saucepan and add fresh water to cover. Add salt and pepper to taste, bring to the boil and simmer for half an hour. Add the sliced onions and potatoes and simmer for a further hour until the potatoes and tender and broken. The water should just cover the meat when it is pressed down. Allow to stand and cool, and skim off all fat. Bring to the boil before serving, dish up the cutlets and sieve the potatoes and onions to a thick sauce. Pour over the cutlets and serve some of the juice separately. Garnish with chopped parsley.

GLAZED SADDLE OF VEAL

Pre-heat oven to 220°C/425°F or gas mark 7
To serve 10–12:

1 saddle of veal (about 5 lbs/ 2.5 Kg)	2 onions
salt and pepper	1 oz/30 g butter
oil	pinch of dry thyme leaves
1 stick of celery	1 tablespoon of fresh chopped
1 carrot	parsley

For the garnish:

24 small onions	2 carrots, peeled and cut into
1½ oz/45 g butter	matchsticks
1 teaspoon of sugar	1 lb/500 g small French peas
	pinch of dry mint leaves

For the sauce:

kidneys from the veal	pepper, salt and sugar, to taste
1 oz/30 g butter	½ pint/30 cl double cream
1 oz/30 g plain flour	1 glass of port
½ pint/30 cl stock	

A saddle of veal is two loins joined together. Get your butcher to chine it, then remove small pieces of bone and any tough skin. Remove the kidneys too, but reserve these for the sauce.

Rub pepper and salt into the veal and brush the outside with a little oil. Roll up the saddle and tie into shape with string. Cut the cooking vegetables into coarse strips and put into a roasting tin with some butter and the herbs. Cover the saddle with greaseproof paper and place in the oven, pre-heated to 220°C/425°F or gas mark 7, and roast for half an hour. Baste and reduce heat. Continue cooking at the rate of fifteen minutes to the pound, basting frequently.

While the meat is cooking, prepare the garnishing vegetables. Boil the onions in a little salted water with ½ oz/30 g of the butter and half of the sugar. Simmer until the water evaporates and the onions are tender and glazed. Cook the carrots, cut into matchsticks, in the same way with ½ oz/15 g of the butter but without the seasoning. Cook the peas with mint and half a teaspoon of sugar, and glaze with melted butter.

When the meat is ready, place on a hot dish and glaze with the gravy juices.

To make the sauce, cut up the kidneys in thin slices and fry in butter. Add the flour and stir until brown. Pour in the heated stock and boil for ten minutes. Season with pepper, salt and a pinch of sugar. Remove from heat and stir in the cream and port. Place the garnishing vegetables around the veal and serve the sauce separately.

STUFFED LOIN OF VEAL

Pre-heat oven to 220°C/425°F or gas mark 7
To serve 6–8:

1 loin of veal (about 4 lbs/2 Kg)	1 onion, chopped
½ lb/250 g minced pork or pork sausage meat	½ pint/30 cl single cream
4 ozs/180 g breadcrumbs	¼ teaspoon of ground white pepper
1 egg	salt and sugar to taste
2 ozs/60 g finely-chopped fresh parsley	bed of roasting vegetables
	½ pint/30 cl stock

Ask your butcher to chine the meat and remove small pieces of bone and tough skin. Then make a forcemeat by mixing together the minced pork or sausage meat, breadcrumbs, egg, parsley, chopped onion which has been fried, cream and seasoning. Lay the loin out flat and spread the stuffing inside. Roll up, starting from the end where the loin bones are thinnest. Tie both ends with string and brush with oil. Cover a roasting tin with a bed of coarsely-cut vegetables and place the stuffed veal on top. Roast in the oven pre-heated to 220°C/425°F or gas mark 7 for fifteen minutes. Reduce heat and add a little of the stock. Continue cooking for a further fifteen minutes to the pound adding the remaining stock a little at a time and basting frequently.

When ready, remove string and dish up. Remove the vegetables and strain off the gravy from the pan. Serve the gravy separately with fried mushrooms.

GRATINÉE OF VEAL

Pre-heat oven to 180°C/350°F or gas mark 4
To serve 8–10:

2 ozs/60 g plain flour	bed of roasting vegetables
4 eggs	4–5 lbs/2–2.5 Kg breast of veal
7 ozs/200 g breadcrumbs	cut into 8 oz/250 g portions
3 ozs/90 g butter	salt and pepper
2 tablespoons of oil	

Dip the veal in the flour, beaten eggs and then the breadcrumbs. Melt the butter and oil in a roasting tin and cover with a bed of mixed vegetables. Place the veal on top, season, cover with foil and roast in the oven at 180°C/350°F or gas mark 4 for one hour and thirty minutes, basting frequently. Remove foil half an hour before cooking time ends to crisp the veal. Dish up the meat, remove the vegetables, strain off the gravy and serve separately.

BRAISED SHOULDER OF VEAL

To serve 6:

4 lbs/2 Kg shoulder of veal	salt and pepper
2 ozs/60 g butter	2 sprigs of parsley, chopped
1 tablespoon of nut oil	1 sprig of thyme, chopped
1 tablespoon of plain flour	3 onions, sliced

3 tablespoons of tomato purée   ½ pint/30 cl veal stock or water
1 teaspoon of Worcester sauce

Cut veal into 6 ozs/175 g portions. Melt the butter and oil in a saucepan. Sprinkle flour and seasoning over the meat and brown on both sides. Add the herbs, onions, tomato purée and Worcester sauce and mix well. Add the hot stock or water and stir until well mixed. Cover the pan and simmer for two hours. Dish up and serve the veal in its own sauce.

BOILED SHOULDER OF VEAL WITH PRAWN SAUCE

To serve 6:

1 shoulder of veal   ½ sweet green pepper, sliced
salt   1 sprig of parsley, chopped
12 white peppercorns   2 onions, sliced

For the sauce:
1 small tin of asparagus tips   1 tablespoon of finely-
¾ pint/40 cl veal stock   chopped fresh parsley
2 tablespoons of plain flour   ½ lb/250 g peeled prawns
salt and pepper   1 oz/30 g butter
                                      ¼ pint/15 cl double cream

Ask the butcher to remove the skin from the shoulder and to crack, but not remove, the bones. Place in a saucepan half-filled with water. Bring to the boil and skim. Add salt, peppercorns, sliced pepper, parsley and onions. Cover and simmer until tender.

To make the sauce, strain half the amount of juice from the asparagus tin into the veal stock. Mix the other half with the flour and stir until smooth. Add to the stock and whisk. Season with salt and pepper and add the parsley. Simmer for ten minutes. Add the prawns to the sauce, remove from heat and stir in cold butter and cream.

When the meat is cooked, remove the bones and cut meat in slices. Spread over some of the sauce and garnish with the asparagus tips. Serve the remaining sauce separately.

SAUTÉ OF VEAL WITH ARTICHOKE HEARTS

To serve 8:

8 fillets of veal, one-inch thick   8 artichoke hearts (tinned)
salt and pepper   ½ pint/30 cl green tartare sauce
1 oz/30 g plain flour   (for recipe see page 215)
3 ozs/90 g butter

Flatten the fillets and then toss them in the seasoned flour. Melt the butter in a pan but do not allow to brown. Blanch the fillets on both sides in the butter, then cook right through. Dish up and garnish with an artichoke heart filled with green tartare sauce.

ROULADE DE VEAU

To serve 4–6:

2 ozs/60 g finely-chopped   2 lbs/1 Kg leg of veal cut into
   parsley   one-inch thick slices
4 ozs/125 g butter   ¼ pint/15 cl stock
salt and pepper   ¼ pint/15 cl double cream
                                 pinch of sugar

Mix the parsley, 2 oz/60 g of the butter, pepper and salt together. Flatten the fillets and spread with the parsley butter. Roll up the meat and fasten with string. Fry in remaining butter until light brown, add the stock, cover and simmer for about three-quarters of an hour or until tender. Dish up the meat and remove the string. Add the cream to the gravy in the saucepan and bring to the boil. Season and add a pinch of sugar. Strain over the roulades.

Serve with new potatoes and a crisp salad.

FRICASSÉE OF VEAL

To serve 3–4:

1 lb/500 g shoulder of veal   2 carrots, sliced
1 teaspoon of salt   1 large onion, sliced

1 bay leaf   1 sprig of parsley, chopped
1 sprig of thyme, chopped   5 white peppercorns

For the sauce:
¾ pint/40 cl stock from the veal   1 tablespoon of double cream
1 oz/30 g plain flour   small knob of butter
juice of a lemon   pinch of sugar
1 egg yolk

Cut the veal into pieces, put in a pan with water to cover, add the salt and bring to the boil. Remove the scum, add the sliced vegetables, herbs and peppercorns. Bring to the boil and simmer until well cooked and tender (about one and a half hours).

To make the sauce, strain and thicken the veal stock with the flour and boil for five or six minutes, then add the lemon juice. Mix the egg yolk with the cream and add to the sauce with the butter. Remove from heat and season to taste with a pinch of sugar.

Glaze the veal with some of the sauce and serve the rest separately.

CUTLETS DE VEAU

To serve 4:

4 cutlets of veal, one-inch thick   ½ pint/30 cl chicken or veal
salt and pepper   stock
1 oz/30 g plain flour   1 tablespoon of redcurrant
2 ozs/60 g butter   jelly
½ lb/250 g mushrooms, sliced   ¼ pint/15 cl double cream

Season the cutlets with salt and pepper and dip in the flour. Fry in the butter for fifteen minutes until golden-brown. Remove and toss the sliced mushrooms in the butter to brown. Return the cutlets to the pan, add the stock and whisk to a smooth consistency. Add the redcurrant jelly and the cream. Simmer for five minutes. Strain the sauce over the cutlets.

FRICANDEAU OF VEAL

To serve 4–6:

1 stick of celery	salt and pepper to taste
1 onion	2 ozs/60 g bacon, cut in strips
2 carrots	2 ozs/60 g butter
2 lbs/1 Kg veal slices from the leg	1 pint/60 cl veal stock
	1 sprig of parsley

Clean and cut the celery lengthways. Peel and cut the onion in quarters. Slice the carrots. Pound and flatten the meat and season with salt and pepper. Roll up the slices of veal with a strip of bacon inside and tie with string. Lightly brown the veal in butter in a frying pan. Put the cut vegetables in a casserole dish and place the veal on top. Whisk out the frying pan with half of the stock and strain over the veal. Cover and braise for half an hour. Then turn the veal, add more stock, cover and braise until tender.

Serve with plain boiled rice, garnished with parsley.

CUTLETS DE VEAU WITH SPAGHETTI

Pre-heat oven to 180°C/350°F or gas mark 4
To serve 6:

6 veal cutlets	6 tablespoons of fresh breadcrumbs
salt and pepper to taste	1 oz/30 g butter
2 tablespoons of plain flour	
2 eggs	

Spaghetti with cheese sauce:

½ lb/250 g spaghetti	3 ozs/90 g grated Parmesan cheese
salt	¼ pint/15 cl tomato sauce (for recipe see page 217)
1 oz/30 g butter	
cayenne pepper	

Season the cutlets with salt and pepper and then coat with the flour. Dip in the egg and then breadcrumbs and fry in butter on a gentle heat until light brown. Place the cutlets in a roasting tin with a few knobs of butter. Cook in the oven pre-heated to 180°C/350°F or gas mark 4 for about fifteen minutes or until tender.

Meanwhile break the spaghetti in half, place in boiling salted water and boil for fifteen to twenty minutes. Drain off the water and wash in cold water. Drain again and put back in the pan with the butter and a pinch of cayenne pepper. Stir lightly and heat. Add 1 oz/30 g of the cheese and the tomato sauce. Mix together.

Dish up the spaghetti on a serving dish, and place the cutlets on top. Serve grated cheese separately.

FRIKADELLER

To serve 4–6:

½ lb/250 g raw veal	2 pints/1.25 litres veal or
½ lb/250 g raw chicken meat	chicken stock
3 tablespoons of breadcrumbs	1 tablespoon of plain flour
½ pint/30 cl single cream	1 egg yolk
2 eggs	juice of ½ lemon
1 teaspoon of salt	1 teaspoon of caster sugar
½ teaspoon of pepper	

I do not believe in nursery meals being dull, but often children develop a craze for a particular dish and you have to keep repeating it until you can interest them in something else. When Prince Charles was a little boy it was meat balls made from chicken or veal. At that time he loved using the house telephone, much to the confusion of the office staff, and he would frequently call me in the kitchen and ask for meat balls. These meat balls – dignified under the Swedish name of Frikadeller – are a classic dish and can be used in a variety of ways. Floated on a dish of clear consommé, for instance, they make a smart dinner party first course.

Put the meat through the mincer three times. Soften the breadcrumbs with 4 fl oz/10 cl of the cream and add to the meat in a basin. Add as much cream again and two eggs, stirring all the time. Season with salt and pepper and roll into small balls. Heat the stock to boiling point and drop in the frikadellers. Boil in batches for fifteen minutes and remove with a straining spoon. Keep hot.

Boil down the stock to about half a pint (30 cl). Mix the flour with some water to form a thin paste. Thicken the stock with the flour mixture, reduce the heat and add the rest of the cream, the egg yolk, lemon juice and sugar. Pour over the frikadellers.

BRAISED VEAL IN THE SWEDISH MANNER

To serve 6:

2 lbs/1 Kg leg of veal	1 large onion, sliced
2 ozs/60 g butter	2 sprigs of parsley
½ pint/30 cl veal stock	1 clove of garlic
1 carrot, sliced	salt and pepper

For the sauce:

1 tablespoon of plain flour	1 tablespoon of redcurrant
16 fl oz/45 cl milk	jelly
	2 tablespoons of double cream

Tie up the boned veal with string and braise in butter until brown. Add the veal stock, sliced carrot, onion, parsley and the clove of garlic. Season well with salt and pepper. Cover the pan and cook slowly for one and a half hours. When cooked remove meat and untie the string. Remove the vegetables and reduce the gravy by boiling for ten minutes. Glaze the meat with a little of the gravy and keep hot.

To make the sauce, dilute the flour in the milk and add to the boiling veal gravy, stirring well. When thickened, strain the gravy into a small saucepan and add the redcurrant jelly. When well absorbed, stir in the cream. Serve separately.

I recommend an accompaniment of lettuce and cucumber salad with a vinegar dressing and small boiled potatoes braised in butter.

VEAL CUTLETS FARCIE

To serve 6:

2 lbs/1 Kg of veal from the leg	½ teaspoon of sugar
4 ozs/125 g fresh breadcrumbs	pinch of nutmeg
4 fl oz/10 cl warm milk	2 ozs/60 g butter
2 eggs	stock, made with the veal bone
salt and pepper	4 fl oz/10 cl white wine

Cut the meat from the leg and use the bone for making stock. Put the meat twice through the mincer. Mix the breadcrumbs with the milk and work the mixture into the meat. Add the beaten eggs, salt and pepper, sugar and nutmeg. Mix well and mould into cutlets. Fry in butter on both sides for ten minutes. Add more butter to the frying pan if necessary, then pour in a dash of stock and the wine. Boil rapidly to reduce the quantity and pour some onto the cutlets. Serve the rest separately.

Dish up with plain boiled rice and button mushrooms sautéed in butter. Instead of a cooked vegetable, try a cucumber salad.

JELLIED VEAL

Pre-heat oven to 220°C/°425°F or gas mark 7
To serve 6–8:

2 lbs/ 1 Kg leg of veal, boned and rolled	pepper
1 tablespoon of oil	2 ozs/60 g butter
garlic salt	½ pint/30 cl veal stock

Rub the veal with the oil and garlic salt. Sprinkle with pepper. Roast the veal in the butter for an hour and fifteen minutes in the oven pre-heated to 220°C/425°F or gas mark 7. After the first fifteen minutes add a quarter of a pint (15 cl) of the stock and baste. Baste every fifteen minutes. When cooked, remove the veal and let it cool. Add the rest of the stock to the pan, bring to the boil, stir and strain into a basin. Let the stock settle into a jelly. Cut the veal into thin slices, bend them and arrange on a dish. Cut up the jelly and sprinkle over the veal.

Decorate the dish with lettuce, sliced cucumber, small artichoke hearts, stuffed olives and mushrooms braised in butter.

Serve with cranberry jelly and a potato salad.

SCHNITZEL DE VEAU AU DIPLOMAT

Pre-heat oven to 180°C/350°F or gas mark 4
To serve 6:

6 cutlets of veal, free from skin and bones, about one-inch thick	1 tablespoon of oil
	3½ ozs/100 g butter
	½ pint/30 cl veal or chicken stock
salt and pepper	¼ pint/15 cl white wine
1 oz/30 g plain flour	¼ pint/15 cl double cream
2 eggs	sugar
4 oz/125 g fresh breadcrumbs	

To decorate:

6 anchovy fillets	chopped capers
6 slices lemon	watercress

Flatten the cutlets and score lightly with a knife on both sides. Sprinkle with salt and pepper, dip in flour and coat with egg and breadcrumbs. Fry over a gentle heat in oil and 3 ozs/90 g of the butter until light brown on both sides. Add the heated stock mixed with half the wine and place in the oven pre-heated to 180°C/350°F or gas mark 4 and cook for fifteen to twenty minutes. Dish up the schnitzels and add the rest of the wine, the cream, sugar and two anchovy fillets to the sauce. Stir over a low heat and mix well. Add a little more stock if necessary.

Strain the sauce, which should be fairly thick, into a pan. Add the rest of the butter, bring to the boil and pour over the schnitzels. Arrange the anchovy fillets in a ring in the centre of the lemon slices and fill with chopped capers. Then place on each schnitzel.

Garnish with a bunch of watercress.

Glazed saddle of veal (p. 86)

SPICED PORK WITH STUFFED CUCUMBER

Pre-heat oven to 220°C/425°F or gas mark 7
To serve 8:

4 lb/2 Kg leg of pork	1 cucumber
salt and pepper	1 lb/500 g cooked spinach
4 tablespoons of brown sugar	1 glass of Madeira wine
8 cloves	1 teaspoon of mixed mustard
¾ pint/40 cl stock, made from pork bones	¼ teaspoon of cinnamon
	2 tablespoons of tomato purée

Rinse the pork in scalding water and score the rind with a sharp knife, then dry thoroughly. Rub salt, pepper and half the sugar into the meat and let it stand for one hour. Insert the cloves between the scored rind and roast the meat for one hour and twenty minutes in the oven, pre-heated to 220°C/425°F or gas mark 7. After the first fifteen minutes add the hot stock and baste. Baste every fifteen minutes.

Peel and cut the cucumber into two-inch long pieces. Boil in salted water for ten minutes, then dry on a cloth. Remove the seeds and stuff with cooked spinach.

When the meat is cooked, remove the rind and cloves, skim the fat from the gravy and place the pork on a dish. Add the wine to the gravy, then the mixed mustard, cinnamon, two tablespoons of sugar and the tomato purée. Boil the gravy, reduce to a glaze and strain over the pork.

Serve the meat with the stuffed cucumber and creamed potatoes.

PORK CUTLETS IN PICKLED CUCUMBER SAUCE

Pre-heat oven to 180°C/350°F or gas mark 4
To serve 6:

6 pork cutlets	¼ pint/15 cl stock
salt and pepper	1 tablespoon of tomato purée
2 ozs/60 g butter	3 tablespoons of pickled
6 tablespoons of breadcrumbs	cucumbers

Pound the cutlets and season with salt and pepper. Dip in melted butter,

Sauté of veal with artichoke hearts (p. 90)

then cover with breadcrumbs. Dip in butter again and place under the grill to brown for a few minutes. Put in the oven set at 180°C/350°F or gas mark 4 for about twenty minutes. Then place on a serving dish. Add the stock and tomato purée to the juice from the pork cutlets. Cut up the pickled cucumber, add to the sauce and bring to the boil. Pour over the cutlets.

STUFFED SPARERIBS OF PORK

Pre-heat oven to 180°C/350°F or gas mark 4
To serve 4:

4 lbs/2 Kg sparerib of pork
1 teaspoon of mixed mustard
1 lb/500 g apples, peeled and
   cored
½ lb/250 g dried prunes, soaked

3 or 4 cloves
½ pint/30 cl stock
1 tablespoon of plain flour
salt and pepper

Ask the butcher to break the sparerib bones in two places. Spread mustard over the pork on the side nearest the bone. Fill with the peeled and cored apples and the soaked prunes. Insert cloves and roll up and tie with string. Put in a tin and braise in the oven pre-heated to 180°C/350°F or gas mark 4, adding the stock a little at a time and basting frequently. When cooked, remove string and take out the cloves, prunes and apples. Serve the prunes and apples as a garnish.

    Add the flour to the gravy in the pan, mix well and season to taste. Stir and boil for six minutes. Strain and serve with the pork.

    Serve with apple purée and redcurrant jelly.

BRAISED FILET MIGNON OF PORK

To serve 8:

8 fillets of pork
salt and pepper
2 ozs/60 g butter
1 tablespoon of tomato purée

¼ pint/15 cl milk
¼ pint/15 cl single cream
pinch of sugar

Flatten the fillets and sprinkle with salt and pepper. Fry in butter until brown. Add the tomato purée, milk, cream and sugar and braise for half an hour.

Dish up and strain the sauce over the fillets.

Serve with creamed potatoes and spinach.

MARINADE OF PORK LUCULLUS

Pre-heat oven to 220°C/425°F or gas mark 7
To serve 6:

3½ lbs/5 Kg loin of pork	1 tablespoon of plain flour
1 teaspoon of salt	½ pint/30 cl good stock
½ teaspoon of white pepper	1 tablespoon of redcurrant
½ pint/30 cl dry white wine	jelly
2 ozs/60 g butter	¼ pint/15 cl double cream

Get the butcher to bone the loin and cut away the rind and surplus fat. Rub in salt and pepper. Place in a deep dish and pour over the wine. Soak the fillets for ten to twelve hours, turning occasionally. Put the butter in a roasting tin to brown and turn the meat in the butter. Place in the oven pre-heated to 220°C/425°F or gas mark 7 for 1¾ hours, basting frequently with the marinade. When cooked, remove and keep warm. Add the flour to the gravy in the roasting tin and pour in the stock. Stir and boil until smooth.

Strain into a small saucepan and add the redcurrant jelly. Stir until it dissolves, then stir in the cream. Season to taste.

Serve with small round potatoes fried in butter and Brussels sprouts.

ESCALOPS OF PORK WITH CREAM SAUCE

Pre-heat oven to 180°C/350°F or gas mark 4
To serve 3–4:

1½ lbs/750 g fillet of pork	½ pint/30 cl good stock
2 tablespoons of plain flour	1 tablespoon of white wine
salt and pepper to taste	½ lb/250 g dried prunes, soaked
¼ lb/125 g butter	pinch of sugar

Cut the fillets an inch thick. Dip in flour and season with salt and pepper. Fry in butter until light brown. Place in a casserole dish. Add the stock to the frying pan and stir until smooth. Strain over the escalops, add the wine, the prunes and a pinch of sugar. Cover with the lid and braise in the oven for thirty minutes until tender. When cooked, dish up the fillets in a circle on a hot dish. Place the prunes in the centre of the dish.

Add the cream to the sauce, bring to the boil and pour over the fillets. Serve with redcurrant jelly, green peas, spinach and fried potatoes.

BRAISED CUTLETS OF PORK

Pre-heat oven to 180°C/350°F or gas mark 4
To serve 4–6:

4 or 6 cutlets of pork, cut ½-inch thick	2 sprigs of parsley
salt and pepper	¼ pint/15 cl stock
2 ozs/60 g butter	1 tablespoon of tomato purée
2 carrots, cut in slices lengthways	½ glass of wine
½ onion, cut in thick slices	¼ pint/15 cl double cream
	pinch of sugar

Trim the cutlets and remove unwanted fat. Season with salt and pepper and fry in butter for five minutes until light brown. Place in a roasting tin on the carrots and onion with the parsley.

Add the stock to the frying pan and stir in with the gravy. Add the tomato purée and the wine, stir and bring to the boil. Strain the gravy over the cutlets and place in the oven pre-heated to 180°C/350°F or gas mark 4. Do not cover. Cook for thirty minutes and baste once or twice. When the cutlets are tender, dish up and strain the gravy. Stir the cream into the gravy, add a pinch of sugar and pour over the cutlets.

Serve with apple sauce, creamed potatoes and baked tomatoes.

SCHNITZEL OF PORK À LA SCALA

To serve 4:

1 lb/500 g loin of pork fillet, cut ½-inch thick	6 tablespoons of breadcrumbs
salt and pepper	1 tablespoon of lard
2 tablespoons of plain flour	a little stock
1 egg	slice of orange and redcurrant jelly, to garnish

Pepper and salt the pork. Dip in flour, beaten egg and then coat in breadcrumbs, and fry slowly in the lard until golden-brown for about half an hour. Remove and place in the centre of a serving dish. Whisk out the pan with a little stock. Strain and pour over the pork. Garnish with a slice of orange with redcurrant jelly in the centre.

If you like, pipe a border of sweet potato purée (for recipe see page 144) around the dish. Tomato sauce (for recipe see page 217) makes an excellent accompaniment to this dish. Serve it in a sauce boat.

GLAZED CARRÉ DE PORC WITH ORANGE SAUCE

Pre-heat oven to 220°C/425°F or gas mark 7
To serve 6:

3 lbs/1.5 Kg smoked Danish back bacon, boned and rolled	1 teaspoon of cinnamon
10 white peppercorns	1 tablespoon of caster sugar
3 cloves	2 tablespoons of grated orange rind
1 teaspoon of dry mustard	orange sauce (for recipe see page 218)

For decoration:

3 bananas	1 tablespoon of sherry
½ oz/15 g butter	

Soak the bacon overnight. Then put in a large saucepan, cover with water and bring to the boil. Skim, add the peppercorns and cloves, cover with a lid, reduce heat and simmer for 1½ hours. Remove from the heat and allow to cool in the stock. When cold, remove the skin.

Spread dry mustard over the fat. Mix together the cinnamon and caster sugar and the grated orange rind. Sprinkle over the bacon pressing well into the fat. Place in the oven which has been pre-heated to 220°C/425°F or gas mark 7, until the fat turns a glazed golden-brown.

Cut each banana in half lengthwise, then across. Fry in butter and pour sherry over them. Cut the pork into thin slices and place together again on a dish. Arrange the banana on top.

Make the orange sauce from the recipe on page 218 and serve separately.

BAKED PRAGUE HAM

Pre-heat oven to 220°C/425°F or gas mark 7
To serve 10–12:

4–5 lbs/2–2.5 Kg Prague ham	3 fl ozs/8 cl vinegar
2 lbs/1 Kg shortcrust pastry	1 tablespoon of syrup
(for recipe see page 224)	1 large tin of peas
1 egg yolk diluted in water	12 baby beetroots
1 tin of sauerkraut	$\frac{3}{4}$ pint/40 cl brown sauce
butter	1 glass of sherry
1 onion, chopped	1 tablespoon of tomato purée
$\frac{1}{2}$ pint/30 cl consommé	salt and pepper to taste

This is the most delicious recipe. For a special occasion Prague ham is well worth tracking down, for it is sweet and succulent beyond belief.

Cover ham in water and bring to the boil. Skim, then simmer for fifteen minutes to the pound after boiling. Peel off the rind and drain in a cloth. Allow to cool. Roll out the pastry and when the ham is cold, place it in the centre of the pastry and cover completely. Decorate with cut-out pieces and brush over with egg yolk diluted in water. Place the ham in the oven which has been pre-heated to 220°C/425°F or gas mark 7, and bake until golden-brown.

Braise the sauerkraut for two hours in a little butter with the chopped onion and add the consommé, vinegar and syrup.

Dish up the ham and surround with the sauerkraut, peas and beetroots. Heat the brown sauce, add sherry and tomato purée, season, dilute with a little stock or water if the sauce is too thick, and serve separately.

FARCIE DE JAMBON PAPRIKA

Pre-heat oven to 180°C/350°F or gas mark 4
To serve 6:

¾ oz/20 g butter
1 truffle, peeled and cut into thin slices
5 stuffed olives
1¾ lbs/850 g raw minced pork
4 ozs/125 g minced smoked ham
½ lb/250 g bread panade (for recipe see page 222)

½ lb/250 g puréed mushrooms
1 egg yolk
3 fl ozs/8 cl Madeira wine
½ pint/30 cl double cream
½ pint/30 cl good meat stock
salt and pepper
pinch of sugar
6 slices of smoked bacon

For the stuffed tomatoes:
5 firm tomatoes

8 ozs/250 g peas, cooked and sieved

Grease a round soufflé dish with butter and decorate the bottom with the sliced truffle and olives. Make a forcemeat of the finely-minced pork and ham and the bread panade. Stir in all the other ingredients except the bacon.

Fill the dish with the forcemeat and top with the bacon slices. Place the dish in a tin of water and poach in the oven which has been pre-heated to 180°C/350°F or gas mark 4, for one and a half hours. Turn out when cooked.

Garnish with stuffed tomatoes, made by cutting five firm tomatoes in half, scooping out the seeds and filling with purée of green peas.

GRILLED GAMMON WITH SWEET HORSERADISH SAUCE

To serve 4:

4 gammon rashers, cut ½-inch thick	½ lb/250 g fresh or frozen spinach
2 lbs/1 Kg potatoes	2 cooking apples
2 tablespoons of butter	¼ pint/15 cl water
3 tablespoons of single cream	1 tablespoon of sugar
salt and pepper	1 tablespoon of horseradish sauce (bottled)
1 egg yolk	
4 tomatoes	

Grill the gammon rashers for five minutes on each side. Boil potatoes, drain and mix in a tablespoon of the butter, the cream, seasoning and egg yolk. Beat thoroughly and place in peaks on a large dish with the grilled gammon.

Peel and de-seed the tomatoes, season and put a dot of butter inside each one. Put on the dish and keep warm. Cook the spinach, drain, and add the rest of the butter. Mix well, season and fill the tomatoes with the spinach.

To make the sauce, peel and core the apples, cook in ¼ pint/15 cl of water until soft, and sieve. Add sugar and mix with the horseradish sauce. Serve separately.

DANISH GAMMON

Pre-heat oven to 220°C/425°F or gas mark 7
To serve 8–12:

1 Danish smoked gammon	2 or 3 cloves
1 apple, peeled and cut in four	dry mustard
1 tin of pineapple juice	4 tablespoons of demerara sugar mixed with ½ teaspoon of ground cinnamon
bay leaf	
6 peppercorns	

This is a disarming little dish for a luncheon party. It looks, and is, simple to prepare but there will be pleasant surprises in store.

Soak gammon overnight and scrub skin thoroughly. Cover with water in a large pan, bring to the boil and skim. Add the apple, pineapple juice, bay leaf, peppercorns and cloves, and simmer for thirty-five minutes to the pound. Allow to cool in its own juice overnight. Skin carefully and smear the fat first with dry mustard and then with demerera sugar mixed with cinnamon. Rub well into the fat and then roast in the oven at 220°C/425°F or gas mark 7, for ten to fifteen minutes, or until brown.

BRAISED VENISON

Pre-heat oven to 160°C/325°F or gas mark 3
To serve 8–10:

¾ lb/350 g fat larding bacon
4 lbs/2 Kg fillet of venison
1 oz/30 g butter
1 carrot
1 onion
1 pint/60 cl stock or water

salt, pepper and garlic salt
2 tablespoons of plain flour
2 tablespoons of redcurrant jelly
1 wine glass of burgundy
¼ pint/15 cl double cream

Wrap the larding bacon round the fillets of venison. Melt the butter in a saucepan and brown the meat. Cut up the carrot and onion and put in the pan with the stock or water. Add the salt, pepper and garlic salt and braise in the oven set at 160°/325°F or gas mark 3 for two hours. Remove the meat and vegetables from the pan and skim off the fat. Mix the flour with a little water and stir into the gravy. Let it boil on top of the cooker for a few minutes to reduce the gravy. Strain into another saucepan and add the redcurrant jelly and more stock if necessary. Add the wine and simmer for three minutes. Remove from heat. Dish up the venison and spoon a little of the sauce over it. Stir in the cream with the rest of the sauce and serve separately.

Only the plainest of vegetables, such as small boiled potatoes, peas or beans, are necessary with this dish.

TURKEY LIVER LUNCH

Pre-heat oven to 180°C/350°F or gas mark 4
To serve 2:

2 large turkey livers	salt and pepper
1 large onion	1 tablespoon of plain flour
1 lb/500 g potatoes	6 rashers of streaky bacon
2 ozs/60 g butter	

Turkey livers can be bought by the pound all year round, but in this country they seem to be an unappreciated delicacy. In Sweden, we consider them to have delicate and exceptional flavour and they are always well received.

Clean and cut the turkey livers into slices, rinse and dry well. Chop the onion and cut potatoes into slices. Use 1 oz/30 g of the butter to grease a fireproof dish and line with the sliced potatoes. Sprinkle the onion on top and season.

Melt the rest of the butter and dip the sliced liver first in butter, then in flour. Place liver on top of the potatoes, cut the bacon in strips and place over the liver. Bake in the oven which has been pre-heated to 180°C/350°F or gas mark 4, for half an hour.

KIDNEYS WITH BRANDY

To serve 2:

4 lambs' kidneys	1 tablespoon of tomato sauce
butter	salt and pepper
2 tablespoons of brandy	¼ pint/15 cl creamy milk
1 teaspoon of plain flour	

Cut the kidneys in half and fry them in a little butter. Put them in a saucepan and pour in the brandy. Then set the brandy alight. Add the flour, tomato sauce and seasoning. Mix well and add the milk. Simmer for half an hour.

Serve with boiled rice or creamed potatoes.

BRAISED OXTAIL

To serve 4:

1 oxtail
2 tablespoons of plain flour
salt and pepper
2 carrots, sliced
1 celery bunch, sliced

2 onions, sliced
1 bay leaf
sprig of thyme
sprig of parsley
1 glass of sherry

Trim and cut the oxtail at the joint sections into pieces about two inches long. Remove excess fat and place in a saucepan of boiling water and parboil for ten or fifteen minutes. Strain off the water and wipe each piece dry with a cloth. Sprinkle over flour, salt and pepper and braise in an iron saucepan for a few minutes.

Add the cut up vegetables and braise with the meat for another five or ten minutes, stirring all the time. Cover the meat with warm water, stir and bring to the boil. Remove the scum and add the bay leaf, thyme and parsley. Cover the pan and braise for three or four hours on a low heat. When cooked put the oxtail in a casserole dish, then add a glass of sherry to the gravy remaining in the pan, bring to the boil and strain over the oxtail.

SAUTÉ OF LIVER WITH MUSHROOMS

To serve 2:

6–8 ozs/175–250 g calves' or
   lambs' liver
1 large onion
2 ozs/60 g butter
$\frac{3}{4}$ lb/350 g mushrooms, sliced

1 oz/30 g plain flour
$\frac{1}{4}$ pint/15 cl stock or water
salt and pepper
1 tablespoon of Madeira wine
$\frac{1}{4}$ pint/15 cl double cream

Cut the liver into strips and chop the onion finely. Put the butter in a saucepan on a medium heat and brown the liver. Add the onion and lower the heat. Add the sliced mushrooms and stir. Sprinkle the flour over the mixture and stir the ingredients together. Add the heated stock or water a little at a time and season. Add the wine, stir well and bring to the boil. Lower the heat and simmer for fifteen minutes. Stir in the cream and simmer for a further ten minutes. Serve with rice.

LIVER IN REDCURRANT SAUCE

To serve 4:

1 lb/500 g calves' liver (leave whole)
equal mix of milk and water
½ lb/250 g bacon rashers
2 ozs/60 g butter
salt and pepper
¾ pint/40 cl hot milk
1 tablespoon of redcurrant jelly
1 tablespoon of plain flour
gravy browning (optional)

This is a dish that everyone will enjoy. Simple ingredients, easy to prepare in advance and served with a rich and delicious sauce.

Soak the piece of liver in equal parts of milk and water for half an hour. Drain and dry in a cloth. Tie the bacon rashers round the liver and braise in 1½ ozs/45 g of butter in an iron saucepan over a gentle heat. When brown, add salt and pepper. Put ¼ pint/15 cl of the hot milk into the pan, cover and braise for an hour, turning the liver over at intervals.

Add the rest of the milk a little at a time. When the liver is cooked, take out of the saucepan, untie bacon and keep hot. Add the redcurrant jelly to the gravy with one tablespoon of flour, and mix well over a low heat. Add a little gravy browning if necessary. The sauce should be a creamy, light brown colour. Add a knob of butter and stir.

Cut the liver into thin slices and place on a hot serving dish. Strain some of the sauce over the liver and serve the rest separately. Serve with rice and spring greens and redcurrant jelly.

TONGUE WITH CUMBERLAND SAUCE ROYAL

To serve 6–10:

1 large ox tongue, smoked or pickled in brine
1 apple, peeled and sliced
1 orange, peeled and sliced
2 or 3 cloves
10 peppercorns

Cutlets de veau with spaghetti (p. 92)
OVERLEAF, LEFT: *Fricandeau of veal (p. 92)*
OVERLEAF, RIGHT: *Escalops of pork with cream sauce (p. 99)*

½ pint/30 cl red wine
1 teaspoon of Bovril

chopped aspic, shredded
  lettuce and parsley, to
  garnish

For the Cumberland sauce royal:
3 tablespoons of redcurrant
  jelly
juice of ½ lemon
½ tablespoon of dry English
  mustard

1 tablespoon of thick-cut
  marmalade
1 wine glass of sherry

Order the ox tongue in good time from the butcher so that he can soak it in brine for at least three weeks. The worst disaster that can befall a tongue is that it should be grey, tasteless and insufficiently salted. If you can find a smoked tongue, this is the best of all.

Place tongue in a large saucepan without tying up, and cover with water. Bring to the boil and skim. Add the cut-up apple and orange, cloves and peppercorns, bring to the boil, reduce heat and simmer for four hours or until tongue is tender.

When cooked, carefully remove skin and the small bones in the root of the tongue, and trim. Strain off stock, reserving ¾ pint/40 cl. Replace tongue in the pan and pour over the stock and red wine. Bring to the boil and allow to simmer, turning the tongue so that it cooks twenty minutes each side.

Allow to cool in its juice, then dish up. Arrange the tongue on a plate so that it is slightly arched in the middle. When cold, slice the tongue almost in half, lengthways. Then cut in thin vertical slices so that it is ready for serving. Heat sauce made from stock and red wine and add the Bovril, boil down and reduce to a demi-glaze. Cool slightly and pour over the tongue. Sprinkle some chopped aspic on either side of the glazed tongue. Decorate the dish with a little parsley and lettuce.

To make the sauce, mix all the ingredients together roughly. Serve the Cumberland sauce separately – if you like, present it in a hollowed-out orange.

Glazed carré de porc with orange sauce (p. 101)

The Bird

UNLESS YOU ARE PREPARED TO REAR AND KILL YOUR OWN FARMYARD roosters, or go to the trouble of finding someone who does, you must accept battery chickens which are tender and cheap but lack flavour. This means, therefore, a change of approach in cooking methods. What has disappeared from the chicken must be put back by the cook. You cannot hope just to pop it in the oven and have something super-tasty at the end.

This is how I treat a chicken. First, I flavour it from inside. Always season *inside* the chicken; salt and pepper on the outside makes very little difference. A pat of parsley butter, a squeeze of lemon or some good stuffing means that the delicate juices are used to the best advantage and the bird absorbs the flavour.

Secondly, there is only one way to get the professional look with a roasted chicken, and that is to rub it with oil before it goes in the oven. This means that the finished bird will have that glorious, all-over sheen instead of looking like a patchy brown and white cocker-spaniel. Furthermore, a good rub with oil seals the skin so that the chicken is cooked from inside. Never insult a bird by roasting it in a pan swimming with animal fats. Instead, massage a little vegetable oil all over the skin before cooking, then you won't have to baste so often either.

Some of my recipes ask you to bone the birds. You may regard this as rather finicky but the heap of bones left behind on the plate is never a pleasant sight. Chicken bones have their beauty of course, but only in the stockpot, which is where they belong.

Most professional cooks do some boning. I never once sent a chicken to the table at Clarence House without removing the bones. When I first worked for the late Lord Rothermere I was told that he refused to eat chickens altogether because he hated the bones. I agreed with him because by the time you have dissected a chicken on your plate, the meat has grown cold.

Boning should be done in the kitchen, and is really quite a simple operation. It is not necessary to hack the bird to pieces. After the chicken is cooked, grasp the bones with your fingers, twist sharply and pull out; they will come away quite easily. This additional attention can lend extra pleasure and delight to good food.

GLAZED CHICKEN RISOTTO

Pre-heat oven to 220°C/425°F or gas mark 7
To serve 6:

3 spring chickens weighing about ¾ lb/750 g each	3 rashers of smoked bacon
salt and pepper	3 cloves of garlic
	nut oil

For the risotto:

8 ozs/250 g rice	½ lb/250 g mushrooms, sliced
livers from the 3 chickens	salt and pepper
1 oz/30 g butter	pinch of sugar
4 slices of bacon, chopped	

This is a perfect example of how to cook chicken so that it has that appetizing, glazed appearance.

Clean chickens and dry thoroughly. Season the inside of each with salt and pepper, and insert in each a piece of rolled-up bacon and a clove of garlic. Rub the skins all over with a little nut oil. Put the chickens in a large pan and roast in the oven which has been pre-heated to 220°C/425°F or gas mark 7, until brown on top. Reduce heat, and turn the chickens on their side so that they brown evenly.

Meanwhile boil the rice for twenty minutes. Drain and put on a tray in the oven to dry. Braise the chicken livers in a little butter, add the cut-up bacon and sliced mushrooms. Cut the chickens' livers into small pieces and mix all together with the rice. Season and add a little sugar.

When the chickens are ready, remove from the oven and allow to cool so that you can handle them. Cut cleanly in half and pull out all possible bones without disfiguring the shape. Remove the garlic and stick the chicken halves together with their own juices. Save the rest of the juice from the pan.

Arrange the risotto on a dish and place the chickens on top. Heat the juice left in the roasting pan and glaze the birds with it.

CHICKEN WITH ITALIAN RISOTTO

To serve 6:

1 boiling chicken (about 4–5 lbs/2–2.5 Kg)
½ a lemon
salt
1 carrot
1 onion
½ a celery stick
bouquet garni

½ teaspoon of Mignonette pepper
½ lb/250 g mushrooms
1 oz/30 g butter
2 tablespoons of breadcrumbs
2 teaspoons of cornflour
¾ pint/40 cl chicken stock

For the Italian risotto:

1 onion
1 dessertspoon of olive oil
2 ozs/60 g butter
8 ozs/250 g rice
1¼ pints/¾ litre chicken stock
pinch of saffron

½ glass of wine or brandy
1 tablespoon of tomato purée
dash of cayenne pepper
4 ozs/125 g grated Parmesan cheese
seasoning

When combining chicken meat with other ingredients, it is nearly always preferable to use a boiled chicken. The way it is cooked means that the flesh is more moist and less liable to shrink. Quite a lot of care should be taken in buying the right sort of boiling chicken for, although it is older than a roaster, it is not – or should not be – old. A chicken is fully grown at four months; by six months it should have put on quite a bit of weight. After its first birthday it begins toughening up, and soon becomes fit only for soup.

This is a useful recipe, using a previously-boiled bird. It is good for feeding large numbers and will stretch to that odd extra guest. It is very tasty, and grand enough for a smallish evening party. You can keep it waiting a bit, too.

Rub the chicken with lemon and salt. Cover with water in a large pan and add more salt. Bring to the boil over a medium heat and skim. Add vegetables, bouquet garni and pepper, and bring to the boil again. Reduce heat and simmer for an hour and a half or until the chicken is tender.

To make the risotto, chop onion and fry in the oil and half the amount of butter until light brown. Add rice, stir and cook until it becomes transparent; add the stock and cook for twenty-five minutes. Dissolve the saffron in the wine and add it to the rice with the tomato purée. Season well, add the rest of the butter and lastly some of the Parmesan cheese. Let the risotto stand for a few minutes.

When the chicken is cooked, remove it and strain the stock. Remove bones and skin from the chicken and cut the meat in small pieces. Peel and slice the mushrooms and braise in butter. Add the chicken and breadcrumbs. Dissolve the cornflour in chicken stock, season and pour over. Simmer over a low heat for a few minutes.

Dish up, making a well in the middle of the rice into which you pour the chicken mixture. Sprinkle more cheese over the top.

FRIKADELLER WITH MUSHROOM SAUCE

To serve 6:

½ lb/250 g raw chicken meat	2 eggs
2 ozs/60 g softened butter	salt and pepper
¼ pint/15 cl double cream	pinch of nutmeg
3 ozs/90 g bread panade (for recipe see page 222)	½ teaspoon of sugar
	1 pint/60 cl chicken stock

For the mushroom sauce:

½ lb/250 g mushrooms	salt and pepper
½ pint/30 cl creamy milk	½ teaspoon of sugar
1 tablespoon of plain flour	1 oz/30 g butter
a little chicken stock	

To any Swedish ex-patriate, the word 'frikadeller' conjures up a hundred dreams. Of all the classic ingredients, the frikadeller mixture is perhaps the most versatile. Moulded into small balls and served with a creamy sauce, it is delicious. Used as a stuffing or steamed in the oven as a chicken cream, the mixture takes on another delectable form. I am proud to have introduced one of Sweden's best advertisements to the British Royal Family.

Cut breast from uncooked chicken and mince finely. Put minced chicken into a basin with the softened butter, cream and bread panade and mix very thoroughly. Add the eggs one at a time with seasoning, nutmeg and sugar, stirring for about one minute each time. Mould the mixture into about 30 small round balls and poach in boiling chicken stock for ten to fifteen minutes.

To make the sauce, clean and cut the mushrooms and boil in the milk for five to ten minutes. Mix flour with stock until smooth, then add the milk. Bring to the boil, add seasoning and sugar and simmer for ten minutes on a low heat. Remove from heat and add the cold butter in small lumps. Pour over the frikadellers.

ROYAL FRIKADELLER WITH LOBSTER SAUCE

To serve 5:

½ lb/250 g raw chicken meat
2 ozs/60 g softened butter
3 ozs/90 g bread panade (for recipe see page 222)
¼ pint/15 cl double cream
pinch of nutmeg

½ teaspoon of sugar
2 eggs
salt and pepper
1 pint/60 cl chicken stock
½ pint/125 g frozen peeled prawns

For the lobster sauce:
1 small tin of lobsters
1 tin of lobster soup
¼ pint/15 cl double cream
½ glass of port wine
1 tablespoon of tomato purée

salt and pinch of sugar
cayenne pepper
1 oz/30 g butter
1 oz/30 g Gruyère cheese

Cut the meat from the uncooked chicken and mince very finely. Put minced chicken into a basin with softened butter and bread panade and mix well. Add the cream, nutmeg, sugar and the eggs, one at a time. Season and stir hard. Shape the mixture into ten portions with a tablespoon so that each is about the size of a poached egg. Poach in chicken stock for about fifteen minutes.

Heat the prawns in their own juice. To make the lobster sauce, sieve the tinned lobster from its juice, add the lobster soup and heat slowly. Stir in the cream, wine, tomato purée and seasonings. Bring to the boil, stir well and add butter in small pieces. Remove from heat and add the cheese. The sauce should not be thick and if necessary can be diluted with milk to taste.

Arrange the prawns in the centre of a serving dish and pour over the lobster sauce. Surround with the frikadellers. Serve with rice mixed with chopped-up cooked gammon and garnished with parsley and black olives.

CHICKEN CHAUD-FROID

To serve 6 as a first course:

1 previously boiled chicken
¼ pint/15 cl suprème sauce (for recipe see page 212)
1 truffle, peeled and sliced

1 sweet green pepper, sliced thinly
1 sweet red pepper, sliced thinly
1 pint/60 cl aspic

To garnish:
lettuce
black olives

green pickled tomatoes
tinned peppers

This is what I call one of my Proud Hostess dishes. The chaud-froid sauce, made with suprème sauce and coated with aspic, is not hard to achieve but requires attention to detail and good judgement. The result is satisfyingly grand.

Remove the skin of the boiled chicken, cut out the breasts and divide them into six portions. Cool the suprème sauce so that it is thick, but still liquid.

With two forks dip the chicken portions into the suprème sauce so that they are well coated. Place on a wire tray and decorate artistically with sliced truffle and thin strips of red and green pepper, making flower shapes or whatever takes your fancy. Have the aspic jelly cooled just at setting point and carefully coat the decorated chicken portions. Put in the refrigerator.

Line a silver dish with the rest of the aspic, leaving a little in the bottom of the jug to set. When everything is firmly set, decorate the dish with lettuce leaves, olives and pickled tomatoes. Place the chicken portions on the dish and arrange the tinned peppers cut in halves. Finish by sprinkling here and there a little chopped aspic from the jug.

Serve with Salade Charlotte (for recipe see page 156).

CHICKEN SAUTÉ

To serve 6:

1 chicken
1 oz/30 g butter
5 small onions
¼ lb/125 g bacon, cut into strips
liver from the chicken, sliced

½ lb mushrooms, peeled and
  sliced
1 tablespoon of plain flour
salt and pepper
½ pint/30 cl stock

Joint the chicken and place in a saucepan with the butter to braise until light brown. Add the onions, bacon, the sliced liver of the chicken and the mushrooms. Sprinkle with flour and season. Stir over a high heat, add the stock and mix well. Cover the pan with the lid and simmer gently for one hour.

Serve hot with vegetables in season and boiled rice.

CUTLETS DE POULET SAUTÉ

Pre-heat oven to 180°C/350°F or gas mark 4
To serve 4:

1 large chicken
3 ozs/75 g butter
1 tablespoon of chopped fresh
  parsley
juice of ½ a lemon
salt and pepper
2 tablespoons of plain flour
¼ pint/15 cl chicken or veal
  stock

1 tablespoon of mushroom
  purée
1 tablespoon of Madeira wine
  or sherry
3 fl ozs/8 cl single cream
1 truffle, peeled and sliced
sprig of parsley or watercress
  to garnish

Cut the breast from the chicken and save the rest of the bird for making stock. Cut breasts into two pieces and then pound to flatten. Make into four cutlets, and insert a slit in each.

Cream 1 oz/30g of butter with the parsley, lemon juice and seasoning and stuff each breast with the mixture. Dip the cutlets into flour and fry in 1 oz/30 g of butter over a gentle heat until golden-brown, basting all the time. Put in the oven pre-heated to 180°C/350°F or gas mark 4, and cook for ten or fifteen minutes.

Pour the stock into the pan in which the cutlets have been sautéed and heat. Add the mushroom purée, wine and seasoning. Boil quickly over a high heat. Reduce heat and stir in the remaining butter and cream. Strain and pour over the cutlets. Place a slice of truffle on top of each cutlet and garnish with watercress or parsley.

Serve with fried potatoes and a salad of French beans and one red chilli cut in strips on a bed of lettuce. Sprinkle with French dressing.

BRAISED CHICKEN À LA GOURMAND

To serve 4:

1 spring chicken	½ orange, cut into four pieces with rind
2 sprigs of parsley	
2½ ozs/75 g butter	1 glass of white wine
salt and pepper	1 teaspoon of redcurrant jelly
1 tablespoon of nut oil	½ pint/30 cl double cream
½ pint/30 cl good chicken stock	1 egg yolk
2 sticks of celery	

Rinse and dry but do not truss chicken. Chop parsley and mix with 1 oz/30 g of butter. Season the inside of the chicken and place the parsley butter inside. Melt the rest of the butter and the oil in a saucepan and braise the chicken light brown all over. Lower the heat, cover the saucepan and cook gently for fifteen minutes. Add a little chicken stock, the celery and orange. Cover and braise for a further fifteen minutes, turning the chicken on its side. Add more stock and the wine at intervals of ten minutes. Turn the chicken once more and cook for about one hour.

Remove the chicken and simmer the sauce down to a glaze. Then add the remainder of the liquid and mix in the redcurrant jelly. Strain this sauce into another pan. Add the cream, whisk well and heat the sauce gently, but do not bring it near boiling point. Add the beaten egg yolk. Remove from heat and keep hot, then stir in a knob of butter. Cut chicken into portions and serve with the sauce.

An excellent accompaniment is pimento rice, which is made by mixing in a sliced red or green pepper with a dish of boiled rice.

CHICKEN SAUTÉ PROVENÇALE

To serve 6:

1 chicken (3 lbs/1.5 Kg in weight)
2½ ozs/75 g butter
1 tablespoon of nut oil
plain flour
salt and pepper
½ pint/30 cl chicken stock

¼ pint/15 cl white wine
1 tablespoon of tomato purée
pinch of sugar
¼ pint/15 cl double cream
8 stuffed olives, to garnish

Remove the legs from the chicken, cut away the breast and remove skin. Cut the legs in two at the joint and cut each breast, diagonally, in two. Melt 2 ozs/60 g of butter and the oil in a frying pan. Dip the chicken pieces in flour and fry over a gentle heat for twenty-five to thirty minutes. Add salt and pepper. Allow a longer cooking time for the legs. When cooked, dish up the chicken on a serving dish.

Add the stock to the frying pan, then the wine, tomato purée and a pinch of sugar. Reduce to half the quantity by boiling rapidly. Lower the heat and add the cream and the rest of the butter.

Strain the sauce over the chicken and garnish with the olives.

POUSSINS WITH POMMES AU GRATIN

Pre-heat oven to 220°C/425°F or gas mark 7
To serve 4:

4 tablespoons of nut oil	2 lbs/1 Kg potatoes
1 teaspoon of tomato sauce	2 ozs/60 g butter
1 teaspoon of Bovril	¼ lb/125 g grated Parmesan
salt and pepper	cheese
2 large poussins	bread sauce (for recipe see
	page 216)

Mix the oil, tomato sauce, Bovril and seasoning together in a bowl. Cut the poussins in half and brush with the oil mixture.

Peel and slice the potatoes and place them in a buttered fireproof dish. Sprinkle with pepper and salt and dot knobs of butter on top. Place the cut poussins on a grilling rack and roast in the oven at 220°C/425°F or gas mark 7 for about thirty minutes along with the potatoes. Brush the birds with the oil mixture once or twice during cooking. When cooked, remove and keep hot. Sprinkle cheese on top of the potatoes and let them cook for another ten minutes. Place poussins on top of the potatoes and serve with bread sauce.

POUSSINS ROYAL

Pre-heat oven to 220°C/425°F or gas mark 7
To serve 4:

4 poussins	¼ lb/125 g bread panade (for
salt and pepper	recipe see page 222)
nut oil	½ pint/30 cl single cream
2 tablespoons of chopped fresh	4 egg yolks
parsley	1 tinned truffle, peeled and
2 ozs/60 g butter	finely-chopped, plus the
½ lb/250 g minced veal	juice from the tin
¼ lb/125 g smoked ham	½ pint/30 cl stock

Whenever I think of that great and lovable Prime Minister, the late Sir Winston Churchill, I am reminded of turtle soup. Not that I ever

Chicken chaud-froid (p. 116)
OVERLEAF, LEFT: *Chicken sauté (p. 117)*
OVERLEAF, RIGHT: *Cutlets de poulet sauté (p. 117)*

cooked any for him, but he consumed vast quantities of it and always took it with him when staying away from home. I remember seeing this turtle soup in the refrigerator at Balmoral Castle and being told that he liked to have it in a thermos in his room at night. The trouble was that poor Sir Winston suffered greatly from his teeth at the time and, being unable to tackle ordinary meals, kept his strength up with turtle soup. Unfortunately, therefore, I cannot say with confidence that Sir Winston ever actually *enjoyed* a meal of mine, but here is a dish, part of which at least, might have helped to fortify the turtle soup.

Season the poussins inside and out with salt and pepper. Brush all over with oil and place some parsley inside each one. Place in the oven, which has been pre-heated to 220°C/425°F or gas mark 7, with the butter and cook for forty minutes, basting occasionally.

In the meantime, mince the veal and ham together and mix with the bread panade. Add seasoning to taste. Whisk the cream and egg yolks together and stir very thoroughly. Add the chopped truffle and the juice from the tin. Mix well together to make a forcemeat.

When the poussins are half-cooked, remove from the oven and allow to cool a little. Then cut in half and remove the bones gently. Stuff the poussins with the forcemeat, stick the halves back together, cover with greaseproof paper and return to the oven at a temperature of 180°C/350°F or gas mark 4, for twenty minutes. Then place on a serving dish and decorate with asparagus tips and mushrooms braised in butter.

To make a gravy, skim fat from the juices in the pan, add the stock, bring to the boil, strain and serve separately.

Serve French beans and new potatoes.

BRAISED PHEASANT WITH CELERY

Pre-heat oven to 180°C/350°F or gas mark 4
To serve 4:

1 brace of pheasants	2 pints/1.5 litres good veal or
salt and pepper	beef stock
½ lb/250 g fat bacon rashers	2 ozs/60 g plain flour
4 celery hearts	1 glass of white wine
some sprigs of parsley	¼ pint/15 cl double cream
butter	pinch of sugar

Poussins with pommes au gratin (p. 120)

Anyone who has ever worked for the British Royal Family would know all about game. From the beginning to the end of the shooting season, all the Royal Households would be flooded with the plentiful produce of the estates. It was my job at Clarence House to think of fresh ways of dealing with this rich stream of pheasant, grouse, partridge etc, and I can remember that I was quite pleased when the shooting season was over. Now that I have to buy my game like anyone else, I think longingly of those van-loads of royally-shot birds.

For this recipe, sprinkle the inside of the pheasants with salt and pepper and tie the bacon round the birds. Put them in a saucepan with two celery hearts, chopped parsley and a knob of butter, and brown over a medium heat. Then add ½ pint/30 cl of heated stock, cover the pan and braise for ten minutes over a high heat. Add the rest of the stock and bring to the boil. Put in a covered dish and cook in the oven at 180°C/350°F or gas mark 4 for about thirty minutes. When cooked, remove the birds and reduce the stock to about half the amount over a high heat. Strain the stock and keep hot.

To make the sauce, first cut the two remaining celery hearts and boil in salted water until tender. Drain and braise in butter on a low heat until golden-brown. Cover and keep hot.

Then melt 1 oz/30 g of butter in a saucepan, add the flour, mix well with a whisk and add the stock, gradually bringing to the boil. Lower heat and simmer for five or six minutes. Add the wine and cream, season with salt and pepper and a pinch of sugar. The sauce should be a creamy golden colour. Lastly, stir in a knob of butter.

Cut the breasts from the pheasants and divide each into two portions. Place the braised celery on a serving dish and put the breasts of pheasant on top of the celery. Coat the pheasants with some of the sauce and serve the rest separately.

Serve with redcurrant jelly, plain boiled potatoes in a napkin and a chicory salad with French dressing.

ROULADE OF PHEASANT WITH SMOKED HAM

Pre-heat oven to 220°C/425°F or gas mark 7
To serve 6:

1 pheasant	½ lb/250 g pork sausage meat

liver from the pheasant
¼ pint/15 cl double cream
salt, pepper and sugar to taste

1 lb/500 g raw smoked ham,
  sliced
butter

For the sauce:
¾ pint/40 cl stock made from
  the pheasant bones

1 tablespoon of tomato purée
knob of butter

Skin the pheasant, remove the meat and put through the mincer twice. Mix with the sausage meat. Lightly fry the pheasant liver in butter and mix with the forcemeat. Stir in the cream. Season with salt, pepper and a little sugar.

Remove the rind from the ham and put a tablespoon of creamed pheasant on each slice, and fold into a roll. Put the filled ham in a roasting tin and spread with a little melted butter. Bake in the oven at 220°C/425°F or gas mark 7 for fifteen to twenty minutes.

To make the sauce, reduce the stock made from the pheasant's bones to half by rapid boiling. Add the tomato purée and knob of butter and boil for two minutes over a high heat. Glaze the roulades with the sauce and serve on a hot dish with bouchées filled with cream of spinach and braised celery.

PHEASANT PIE

Pre-heat oven to 220°C/425°F or gas mark 7
To serve 6:

For the pastry:
1 lb/500 g plain flour
2 ozs/60 g lard
6 ozs/175 g butter

2 egg yolks
salt and pepper
water to mix

For the filling:
2 pheasants
¼ lb/125 g fat bacon rashers
butter

1¼ pints/¾ litre veal stock
salt and pepper
½ sweet red pepper

For the sauce:

1 oz/30 g butter
1 tablespoon of plain flour
stock

¼ pint/15 cl double cream
salt, pepper and a pinch of
     sugar

First, make the pastry according to the short pastry recipe on page 224.

Tie the bacon round the birds and braise in butter until light brown. Add ¼ pint/15 cl of stock, season with salt and pepper, cover the saucepan and braise for twenty minutes. Add 1 pint/60 cl more of stock, turn the birds, cover and cook over a gentle heat until they are tender. Remove the birds, cut in half lengthways, remove the bones and put the bones back in the pan with the gravy. Simmer for half an hour. Cut the birds in small portions.

Blanch the pepper in boiling water, remove seeds, cut into strips and mix with the pheasant. Line a pie form with pastry, fill it with the meat and cover with the stock. Put the pastry lid on with some appropriate pastry cut-outs, brush with beaten egg and place in the oven at 220°C/425°F or gas mark 7 for fifteen minutes. Turn down the heat, cover the pie crust and cook for a further thirty minutes. Serve hot or cold.

If serving hot, make the following sauce. Strain the remaining gravy and skim off the fat. Put the butter in a pan, add flour and mix well over the heat until brown. Add some gravy and stir until smooth. Add more gravy and simmer for five minutes. Then add the cream and season with salt, pepper and a pinch of sugar. The sauce should be golden-brown and quite thick.

PARTRIDGES EN CASSEROLE

To serve 4:

¼ lb/125 g minced pork and
     veal, mixed
2 partridges
¼ lb/125 g fat bacon rashers
¼ pint/15 cl chicken stock
1 onion

1 carrot
salt and pepper
½ lb/250 g mushrooms
½ a sweet red or green pepper
butter

Mix the minced pork and veal together to make a forcemeat. Cut the mushrooms in half and the pepper in strips. Stuff the partridges with the forcemeat and tie the bacon fat round them. Braise in a fireproof dish on a gentle heat and add a little stock at intervals. Add the onion, carrot and seasoning. Cover and cook for an hour. Meanwhile, braise the mushrooms in a little butter with the pepper.

When the partridges are cooked, remove them and strain the stock. Remove the bacon and cut the partridges in half. Put them in a clean casserole dish with the pepper and mushrooms and pour the sauce over. Simmer for ten or fifteen minutes.

STUFFED PARTRIDGE

Pre-heat oven to 220°C/425°F or gas mark 7
To serve 4:

2 partridges	1 lb/500 g button mushrooms
salt and pepper	½ lb/250 g sliced bacon
1 lb/500 g minced chicken	good stock
1 tablespoon of oil	1 glass of Madeira wine
1 tablespoon of melted butter	

Cut the partridges in half and remove the backbones. Season well and fill each half with the minced chicken. Stick the partridges together again, place in a roasting tin and coat them with a mixture of oil and melted butter. Roast in the oven at 220°C/425°F or gas mark 7 for twenty-five minutes, basting frequently.

Remove from the oven, divide the halves and serve with quickly-braised mushrooms and rolls of grilled bacon. Make the rest of the chicken into balls, fry them and add to the dish.

Swirl out the pan with some stock, add the Madeira wine and a knob of butter. Heat, reduce the gravy by boiling and strain over the partridges.

WILD DUCK

Pre-heat oven to 220°C/425°F or gas mark 7
To serve 4:

2 small wild duck	salt and pepper
½ lb/250 g mushrooms	¼ pint/15 cl stock
1 onion	1 tablespoon of double cream
butter	1 glass of port wine
1 tablespoon of plain flour	brown breadcrumbs

Roast the wild duck in the oven at 220°C/425°F or gas mark 7 for about twenty-five to thirty minutes. When cooked, remove the breasts, cut in slices lengthways and replace on the breast bones. Remove the legs and cut in two at the joints, then replace. Spoon over some of the gravy from the roasting tin. Skim the fat off the rest of the gravy and keep hot.

Chop up the mushrooms and onion and braise in a little butter for one or two minutes. Add the flour and seasoning and stir over a high heat, pour in the stock and cook until thickened. Then add the cream and the wine and simmer for five minutes. Pour the thick mixture over the breasts of the duck.

Mix the breadcrumbs with a knob of butter and put on top of the ducks. Put in the oven at 150°C/300°F or gas mark 2 for fifteen minutes.

Serve with redcurrant jelly and a sharp salad.

ROAST GROUSE

Pre-heat oven to 230°C/450°F or gas mark 8
To serve 2:

2 young grouse, well hung	¾ pint/40 cl beef stock
fat bacon rashers	brown breadcrumbs

Grouse have their own distinctive flavour and are best cooked plainly.

Tie the birds with bacon fat and roast for fifteen to twenty minutes in the oven at 230°C/450°F or gas mark 8, basting every five minutes. When cooked, cut the grouse in half lengthways and remove the backbones. Boil the bones in the beef stock.

Add a little stock to the roasting pan and stir. Strain into the beef stock. Reduce the stock to half the amount by boiling, and strain. Serve with the grouse. Dish up the birds on a bed of fried brown breadcumbs.

Garnish with straw potatoes and watercress. Serve with bread sauce, French beans and a crisp green salad.

GALANTINE OF GAME

Pre-heat oven to 180°C/350°F or gas mark 4
To serve 6–8 as a first course

1 cooked grouse	1 carrot
1 cooked pheasant	parsley
½ lb/250 g mixed minced pork and veal	salt and pepper
	½ oz/15 g gelatine
1 onion	¼ pint/15 cl red wine

For a party, nothing looks nobler than a beautiful home-made galantine of game.

Cut some fillets from the grouse and pheasant and put to one side. Mince small pieces of game and add to the pork and veal forcemeat and season well. Put the game carcasses in a saucepan with the vegetables, parsley and some seasoning. Cover with water, bring to the boil and simmer for two hours. Strain, and reduce liquid to about 1 pint/60 cl.

Line a terrine dish first with a layer of the game fillets, then with the forcemeat and season between each layer. Leave room in the dish for the liquid to be added later. Place the dish in a tin of hot water and bake in the oven at 180°C/350°F or gas mark 4 for an hour.

Heat the strained stock and dissolve the gelatine in it, add the wine. Allow to cool a little and pour the aspic over the meat in the tin.

When set, turn out on a dish and garnish with any remaining aspic, chopped, and with lettuce and thinly-sliced sweet red pepper.

TERRINE OF GAME

To serve 6–8

1 pheasant	½ teaspoon of salt
2 partridges	¾ lb/350 g shin of veal
2 ozs/60 g butter	3 tablespoons of powdered
3 pints/1.75 litres good stock	aspic
3 cloves	¼ pint/15 cl white wine
8 white peppercorns	2 hard-boiled eggs

Braise the pheasant and partridges in the butter, add stock, cloves, peppercorns and seasoning. Cut the veal into large pieces, wash in hot water and put in the saucepan with the birds. Bring slowly to the boil and skim. Simmer for one and three-quarter hours with the lid on. Remove the birds and meat, and cut the flesh into pieces. Replace the bones in the stock, simmer and reduce to 2 pints/1.25 litres. Remove and cool. Strain the stock and skim off as much fat as possible.

Stir in the aspic powder and dissolve. Add the wine and leave to cool.

Arrange the cut meat in a terrine dish with slices of hard-boiled egg. Then pour over the aspic, cool but not yet set, and leave in a cold place to set.

TURKEY WITH WALNUT STUFFING

Pre-heat oven to 220°C/425°F or gas mark 7
To serve 15:

½ lb/250 g ground walnuts	salt and pepper
butter	2 lbs/900 g sausage meat
¼ lb/125 g breadcrumbs	1 turkey (about 15 lbs/7 Kg)
2 tablespoons of double cream	nut oil

Mix together the walnuts, a knob of butter, breadcrumbs and cream, and season. Stuff the rear end of the turkey with the sausage meat and the neck end with the walnut stuffing.

Rub nut oil all over the skin of the bird. Place in the oven pre-heated to 220°C/425°F or gas mark 7 and roast for fifteen minutes, then baste. When the turkey has turned a light brown colour, reduce the heat, turn on its side and cook for ten to fifteen minutes per pound. Baste and turn the turkey every fifteen minutes.

When cooked, strain the juice and skim off the fat. Garnish with chipolata sausages. Serve with cranberry sauce and bread sauce.

TURKEY AND HAM PIE

Pre-heat oven to 220°C/425°F or gas mark 7
To serve 4:

1½ lbs/750 g leftover turkey and ham
8 ozs/250 g short pastry (for recipe see page 224)

1 pint/60 cl chaud-froid sauce (for recipe see page 219), made from chicken or veal stock
4 hard-boiled eggs

Cut leftover turkey and ham into pieces – chicken too if you have any. Line an 8 inch/20 cm pie tin with short pastry, cover the bottom with sauce, then with the mixed meat. Place the hard-boiled eggs on top and fill up with the rest of the meat. Finish by pouring over the rest of the sauce, then cover with pastry. Decorate with pastry cut-outs, brush with beaten egg and bake in the oven pre-heated to 220°C/425°F or gas mark 7. Reduce the heat after the first fifteen minutes and bake for a further half-hour. Turn out carefully.

ROAST DUCK SCANDINAVIAN STYLE

Pre-heat oven to 220°C/425°F or gas mark 7
To serve 4:

½ lb/250 g veal
½ lb/250 g smoked gammon
6 ozs/175 g bread panade (for recipe see page 222)
1 onion

butter
½ pint/30 cl creamy milk
salt, pepper and sugar to taste
2 young ducks

For the sauce:

1 tablespoon of fat from duck
    gravy
1 tablespoon of plain flour
½ pint/30 cl veal stock
gravy from the duck
raw livers from the ducks
    (sieved)

1 glass of Madeira wine
½ lb/250 g prunes, cooked,
    stoned and chopped
salt and sugar to taste

Mince the veal and gammon twice together and mix with the bread panade. Cut the onion finely and braise in butter, then add to the meat mixture with the milk and seasoning. Mix thoroughly.

Split the ducks open and remove the breast bones. Sprinkle salt and pepper inside and stuff with the forcemeat. Tie the ducks up in their natural shape and cover with foil. Place in the oven pre-heated to 220°C/425°F or gas mark 7, to cook for one hour and fifteen minutes. After an hour, remove the foil, baste the ducks with their own gravy and let them brown for the remaining fifteen minutes. Place on a serving dish to keep hot.

To make the sauce, remove fat from the gravy and put 1 tablespoon of the fat into a saucepan. Add the flour to the duck fat, pour in the stock, stir well, add the duck gravy and the livers. Cook for five minutes. Add the wine and the prunes and season with salt and sugar. Simmer for ten minutes.

Dish up the ducks on a serving dish and serve with green peas mixed with sweet red peppers cut in strips and cream potatoes. Serve the sauce separately and redcurrant jelly.

ROAST DUCKLING

Pre-heat oven to 220°C/425°F or gas mark 7
To serve 4–6:

2 ducklings
liver from the ducklings
salt and pepper

3 dessert apples, sliced
½ lb/250 g dried prunes, soaked

For the sauce:

2 tablespoons of plain flour
juice from the roasted
  ducklings
½ pint/30 cl beef stock

1 glass of sherry
1 tablespoon of redcurrant
  jelly
salt and pepper to taste

Rub the breasts of the ducklings with the liver, sprinkle inside and out with salt and pepper and stuff with the cut-up apples and the prunes.

Roast in the oven which has been pre-heated to 220°C/425°F or gas mark 7, basting every fifteen minutes. After the first fifteen minutes, lower the heat and continue roasting for one hour and fifteen minutes. When ready, the skin should be crisp and light brown. Remove from the oven and keep hot.

To make the sauce, add flour to the juice from the ducklings and stir well. Add the heated stock, stir until smooth and add the wine, redcurrant jelly and seasoning. If the sauce is thick, add a little more stock and some juice from the prunes. Taste, adjust seasoning and strain. Serve separately with the ducklings.

ROAST DUCK SUÉDOISE

Pre-heat oven to 220°C/425°F or gas mark 7
To serve 4–6:

1 lb/500 g dried prunes
2 dessert apples
2 cloves

1 duck
salt and pepper

For the sauce:

skimmed gravy from the
  cooking juices
1 tablespoon of plain flour
½ pint/30 cl stock (preferably
  beef)

½ glass of prune juice
1 glass of claret
1 dessertspoon of orange
  marmalade

Soak the prunes overnight in cold water and remove the stones. Core and quarter the apples and insert the cloves. Season the duck generously with salt and pepper, inside and out. Rub the breast with the liver from the bird.

Stuff the duck with the apples and half the prunes. Cover the breast with buttered greaseproof paper and roast in the oven, which has been pre-heated to 220°C/425°F or gas mark 7, for an hour and twenty minutes. Lower the heat after the first half hour and baste occasionally. Remove the paper fifteen minutes before the cooking time is up, and let the duck brown without basting.

While the duck is cooking, simmer the remaining prunes in water until soft. When cooked, add a pinch of salt and keep simmering on a low heat.

When the duck is cooked, remove from the oven, place on a dish and keep warm. Skim the fat from the gravy in the pan. To make the sauce, add flour to the skimmed gravy, and stir until smooth. Add the stock and simmer for ten minutes. Add the prune juice, half the glass of claret and the marmalade. Check seasoning, strain and keep hot.

To garnish, pour a tablespoon of the fat from the duck on to the strained prunes, add the rest of the claret and simmer for a few minutes so that the prunes become glazed. Arrange them round the duck.

Serve with red cabbage and new potatoes.

ROAST GOOSE WITH FRUIT STUFFING

Pre-heat oven to 220°C/425°F or gas mark 7
To serve 10:

1 goose, about 8 lbs/4 Kg	1 orange
½ a lemon	1 lb/500 g dried prunes, stoned
salt and pepper	1 small tin of pineapple cubes
2 dessert apples	1 tablespoon of port wine
2 or 3 cloves	

For the sauce:

juice from the roasting pan, skimmed of all fat	1 tablespoon of redcurrant jelly
1 teaspoon of cornflour	salt and pepper
1 glass of red wine	giblets from the goose, minced
1 tablespoon of orange marmalade	

Soak the prunes in warm water until swollen, then remove the stones.

Rub the goose inside and out with the lemon. Season inside with salt and pepper. Cut the apples in quarters and stick with cloves. Quarter the orange, leaving the skin but removing the pips.

Stuff the goose with the orange and apples and half the stoned prunes. Close the opening with a skewer. Roast in the oven which has been pre-heated to 220°C/425°F or gas mark 7, for twenty minutes. Lower the heat and cook for one and three-quarter to two hours, basting every ten minutes.

When cooked, serve on a dish garnished with pineapple cubes and the rest of the prunes which have been previously cooked in water with a tablespoon of port wine and reduced to a glaze. Cut the breast of the goose in slices from the top and replace into its natural shape.

To make the sauce, thicken the juice from the roasting pan with the cornflour and add the wine, marmalade and redcurrant jelly. Season and simmer. Then add the minced giblets to the gravy. Simmer for five minutes and serve with the meat.

Vegetables and Salads

UNTIL I WAS ABOUT THIRTY I HAD NEVER BOUGHT A VEGETABLE – I always picked them. I worked in the huge, beautiful and rather feudal castles in Sweden, which were entirely self-supporting estates. I snatched little beetroots from the earth, dashing the hopes of the gardeners who wanted them to grow to exhibition size, and then pickled them to my own recipes. Any housewife will appreciate the deep and simple satisfaction I felt when gazing at a cellar full of peaches and pears which had taken a week to bottle.

I learned the right way of using everything that came out of the earth, and with it a deep respect for the order and rhythm of life.

Nowadays most people have forgotten the pleasure of picking vegetables in season. But there must be something missing, or the advertisers would not find it necessary to spend good money designing green packets and describing the exact moment the pod went pop!

I grow only a few of my own vegetables now. I appreciate what can be bought in convenient cans and packages, and make full use of them, while at the same time being rather choosey about brands. It is not the amount of tinned and frozen vegetables sold that worries me, but the increasing narrowness of attitude towards what fresh produce is available. Something is wrong when housewives ignore fresh spring cabbage –as tender as asparagus if properly treated – in favour of frozen peas. Have they forgotten the beauty of the Jerusalem artichoke which proves its goodness by the jellied stock it leaves in the pan? There is nothing more delicious than French beans in season; make a great fuss of them and serve as a separate course for a dinner party or as a special dish for a lunch party.

Everyone has their own way of cooking vegetables, of course, and people do not usually compare recipes on how to cook, say, Brussels sprouts. However, I feel such things are important for it is surprising how often vegetables are overcooked: time runs away when cooking a meal and the poor old vegetables are not rescued until soft and mushy. When this happens, you might as well drink the cooking water, for the vegetables will have lost all their Vitamin C, and will look most unappetising too. Leaving the lid off the pan is another way of wasting the nutrients.

Vegetables properly cooked and appetisingly served and garnished, will go a long way to boosting the morale of any dish – and will do you a lot of good too.

You will see that I have first listed a number of vegetables and given you advice on how they should be prepared and served as accompaniments to main courses. More elaborate recipes for vegetables and salads, some of which form meals in themselves, follow.

BEANS, BROAD

Pod the beans. Boil in salted water for five minutes with the lid on. Drain and remove the skins, put back in the saucepan with a lump of butter, cover and simmer for five to ten minutes. Add half a tablespoon of chopped parsley and a pinch of sugar.

BEANS, FRENCH

Top and tail the beans, rinse and tie them into bundles. Place in salted boiling water with a pinch of soda. Boil until tender, about ten to twelve minutes, but do not overcook. Drain and wash over with cold water, then place on a cloth to drain.

BRUSSELS SPROUTS

Cut off any wayward outer leaves and slice the ends off the stalks. Cross with a knife. Put in cold water for half an hour, so as to get rid of any foreign bodies.

Plunge into *boiling* salted water and whatever anyone tells you, there is nothing wrong with that old cook's trick of adding a pinch of soda; it makes them remain green instead of going grey. Bring up to the boil again and lower the heat considerably. Let them stand in this simmering, not boiling, water for fifteen minutes until they sink down and are still nutty. It is all the hectic boiling that makes them mushy. Keep the lid on all the time.

Strain very thoroughly and then return to the empty saucepan adding some butter. Swirl the sprouts in the butter and dish up.

Alternatively, you could prepare sprouts as above, dry in a cloth and then fry gently in butter until golden-brown. They are delicious like this too.

CABBAGE

Cut cabbage in half and remove the outer leaves. Cut out the stalk and pare off some of the thick veins. Leave in cold water for fifteen minutes.

Then put in boiling salted water; push the leaves down so that the water almost covers. Add a pinch of soda and cook for ten minutes with the lid on. When cooked, drain very thoroughly, pressing the cabbage gently with a plate to rid it of excess water. Spread some butter inside and roll up.

CARROTS

Top and tail, scrape and cut downwards in fairly thin sticks; then cut the sticks in half. Just cover in plain water and boil quickly so that the water evaporates. When all the water has gone the carrots are cooked. If any excess water is left, drain it off and add half a tablespoon of butter to the carrots in the pan; swirl the carrots around in the steam, add pinches of salt, pepper and sugar and glaze the carrots in the butter.

Salt in the cooking water causes carrots to discolour.

CARROTS VICHY IN WINE

Scrape small, new carrots. Boil in a little water until tender, strain off, add a knob of butter, sugar to taste and half a glass of white wine. Cooked in this way, they are a delicious garnish to a main meal.

CAULIFLOWER

Cut off the stalk and divide the cauliflower into sprigs. Choose a few good leaves and dice the tender part of the stalk if desired. Soak in cold water for a few minutes.

Put in the pan enough boiling salted water to cover the cauliflower and cook rapidly for ten minutes or less with the lid off. Unfortunately, cauliflower produces an unpleasant smell which permeates the vegetable if the lid is left on. Drain in a cloth and serve with melted butter.

CELERY, BRAISED

Clean and cut a celery heart in half, boil in salted water until tender. Drain on a cloth, cut each half in two pieces and braise in butter until golden.

GLOBE ARTICHOKES

These look a little like thistles; the short ones are the best. Cut off all the thorny bits at the top of the leaves and level the roots. Soak in cold water for one hour to get rid of any bitterness.

Place in about 3 pints/180 cl of boiling salted water in a deep pan with a pinch of soda to keep from greying. Boil for twenty minutes to half an hour with the lid on. Test for readiness by pulling a leaf – if it comes away easily the artichokes are done. Drain, head down, in a cloth and keep warm. Serve on a napkin with melted or creamed butter, and a little lemon juice served separately.

JERUSALEM ARTICHOKES

These are a bit of a bother to peel, but persevere until the artichokes are clean and white. Put in cold water for a few minutes. Then boil in salted water for ten or fifteen minutes.

Strain and serve with knobs of butter on top. Don't whatever you do throw away the cooking water as it is wonderful for soups. Watch it jellify in the pan.

PURPLE SPROUTING BROCCOLI

Remove any pieces you don't like. Then chop up the stalks so that all pieces of the broccoli are the same length. Tie up in bundles and leave in cold water for half an hour.

Boil for twenty minutes in just enough water to cover, adding a small piece of garlic, salt and a pinch of soda. When cooked, drain carefully and put in a cloth until wanted. Serve with melted butter.

SEA-KALE

Trim and remove the root, rinse well and tie in bundles. Boil in enough salted water to cover with the lid on for ten minutes. Remove, drain and serve with melted butter. If you add crisply-fried pieces of bacon, this can be a course in itself.

SPINACH

Pick over the spinach very carefully, removing coarse veins. Soak in lots of cold water to get rid of all the grit.

Put very, very little water in the saucepan, just enough to cover the bottom of the pan. Add salt and a pinch of bicarbonate of soda to make it cook quicker. Pack the spinach well down in the pan and start cooking at a moderate temperature, increasing the pace after the first five minutes. Cook for about fifteen minutes, or until spinach is tender. Remove the lid during the last five minutes to let surplus moisture evaporate. To serve, roll the leaves up and sprinkle them with melted butter.

Potatoes are the most versatile of all vegetables. It saddens me when I hear people dismiss them by saying they are fattening. *Any* food is fattening if you eat too much of it. I have eaten potatoes all my life and I am not fat. Her Majesty the Queen always eats potatoes and retains a wonderful figure. Try some of the following dishes and you will see just what I mean about potatoes being versatile.

POTATO SOUFFLÉ

To serve 4:

1 egg	salt and pepper
½ lb/250 g potatoes, mashed	6 medium-sized tomatoes
2 rashers fried bacon, cut up	¼ lb/125 g Gruyère cheese,
1 onion, finely-chopped	grated

Beat in the egg with the mashed potatoes and add the cut-up fried bacon, the chopped onion and salt and pepper. Cut the tops off the tomatoes and remove the seeds. Fill the tomatoes with the potato mixture. Sprinkle with cheese and place in a hot oven for ten minutes.

Delicious with roast lamb.

SPECIAL DUCHESSE POTATOES

To serve 2–4:

½ lb/250 g potatoes, mashed
1 tablespoon of cold butter
1 egg

¼ lb/125 g chopped and fried
   mushrooms
salt, pepper and sugar
ground almonds

Mix the potatoes, 1 tablespoon of cold butter, egg, mushrooms, seasoning and a pinch of sugar, and shape into small balls. Roll in ground almonds and fry in butter until light brown.

Wonderful with chicken.

BAKED POTATOES BOHEMIAN

1 potato per person
2 tablespoons of sausage meat
   per person

salt and pepper
butter
tomato purée

This is a useful supper dish when faced with a gang of hungry teenagers, or an unexpected guest. Highly popular with the children too.

Bake large potatoes in their jackets, cut a lid and scoop out the inside. Mash the scooped-out potato, mix with sausage meat, and season. Replace the mixture in the jackets and brush the top with melted butter and a little tomato purée mixed together. Bake in the oven for twenty minutes.

POTATO PANCAKES

To serve 2–4:

1 lb/500 g potatoes
2 or 3 tablespoons of plain
    flour
2 tablespoons of milk

1 egg
salt and pepper to taste
½ lb/250 g green bacon or pork

Wash, peel and grate the potatoes into a basin. In another basin, mix the flour, milk and egg to a smooth paste. Season, and add to the grated potatoes. Cut the bacon or pork into small pieces and fry gently until golden-brown. Add to the mixture. Using about two tablespoons of the mixture at a time, shape into small pancakes and fry in bacon fat. Allow the mixture to set on top before turning to fry on the other side.

    This is delicious served hot and golden with cranberry sauce and watercress salad.

STUFFED POTATO DUMPLINGS

To serve 6:

1 lb/500 g potatoes, mashed
    (cold and seasoned)
2 eggs

6 ozs/175 g plain flour
1 onion
½ lb/250 g bacon

Add to the cold seasoned potato the eggs and 4 ozs/125 g of the flour and mix to a dough. Pat the dough on a floured board and work in the rest of the flour.

    Fry the chopped-up onion and bacon gently until brown and remove from pan. Roll the potato dough into a loaf and cut into pieces the size of medium potatoes. Roll out and stuff each one with the bacon and onion mixture. Shape into dumplings. Have ready 3 pints/180 cl of boiling salted water and drop dumplings in a covered pan. When they rise to the surface, they are cooked. Remove with a draining spoon and serve with melted butter.

POTATO MIGNON

To serve 4:

1 lb/500 g potatoes, mashed
2 eggs
butter

pepper, salt and sugar to taste
plain flour

Mix the potatoes, eggs, butter and seasoning together and roll into cakes one inch thick. Roll in flour and fry in butter until light brown.
  Good served with fried bacon.

POTATOES MACRÉE

To serve 4:

1 lb/500 g potatoes, boiled in their skins
1 oz/30 g butter

1 onion, sliced
salt and pepper

Peel the cooked potatoes, cut in slices and fry in butter with the onion. Season and fry gently until brown.

PARSLEY POTATOES

To serve 4:

1 lb/500 g potatoes, boiled
½ pint/30 cl béchamel sauce (for recipe, see page 211)
knob of butter

1 tablespoon of chopped fresh parsley
salt, pepper and sugar

Cut potatoes into cubes. Heat the béchamel sauce and add the butter, parsley and seasoning. Mix in with the potatoes.
  Good with salt beef.

SCANDINAVIAN POTATO BALLS

To serve 4:

1 lb/500 g potatoes, boiled in
    their skins

2 ozs/60 g butter or bacon fat
salt, pepper and sugar to taste
brown breadcrumbs

Peel potatoes and shape into balls. Fry in butter, add salt and pepper and
enough breadcrumbs to coat. Stir and turn gently over a low heat.
When golden, sprinkle a little sugar on top and serve.

NEW POTATOES

To serve 6–8:

2 lbs/1 Kg new potatoes
salt

mint
a knob of butter

Wash and scrape the potatoes, place in salted, boiling water with a sprig
of mint, cover and cook for fifteen minutes. Strain off the water, replace
on low heat to dry and add the knob of butter. Keep some fresh mint
aside for decoration and serve in a hot dish.

POTATOES SUÉDOISE

To serve 6–8:

2 lbs/1 Kg potatoes
¼ lb/125 g butter

salt, pepper and sugar to taste

Peel the potatoes and cut in boat-shaped quarters. Melt the butter in a
baking tin and add the potatoes, spinkle with pepper and salt and bake in
the oven until they are light brown. When cooked, sprinkle a little sugar
on top and serve.

PURÉE OF SWEET POTATOES

To serve 6–8:

2 lbs/1 Kg sweet potatoes
1 tablespoon of butter

1 tablespoon of double cream
pinch of cayenne pepper

Sweet potatoes can be bought at most high-class greengrocers and supermarkets. They have a slightly sweet taste which goes particularly well with pork. Simply cook in the same way as ordinary potatoes. Mash, add butter, cream and pepper and beat very thoroughly.

HARICOTS VERTS À LA CRÈME

To serve 6–8:

2 lbs/1 Kg French beans
salted water
3 fl oz/8 cl wine vinegar
2 egg yolks

½ pint/30 cl single cream
juice of ½ a lemon
1 oz/30 g cold butter
chopped fresh parsley

Top and tail the beans, remove strings, tie into bundles and boil in salted water for ten minutes.

Make the sauce by boiling and reducing the vinegar to a third of the quantity. Remove from heat. Whip the egg yolks and cream in another saucepan over a gentle heat until thickened. Remove from heat and add the lemon juice and vinegar in small quantities. Lastly, whisk in the butter (slightly softened, but cold) in small lumps. Keep hot. Pour the sauce over the beans and sprinkle with chopped parsley.

SAVOURY FRENCH BEANS

To serve 6–8:

2 lbs/1 Kg French beans
salted water
½ oz/15 g melted butter
1 clove of garlic, crushed

2 tablespoons of grated
    Parmesan cheese
fried bacon, cut in strips

Pheasant pie (p. 123)
OVERLEAF, LEFT: *Stuffed partridge (p. 125)*
OVERLEAF, RIGHT: *Roast grouse (p. 126)*

Top and tail the beans and boil in salted water for ten minutes. Drain on a cloth. Fry the beans in butter with the garlic, sprinkle with the grated cheese and fry for two minutes over a low heat.

Serve very hot with strips of fried bacon sprinkled on top.

CHICORY IN CREAM SAUCE

To serve 3:

6 whole chicory	2 tablespoons of grated
salted water	Gruyère cheese
2 egg yolks	½ pint/30 cl single cream
pinch of cayenne pepper	

Chicory, the small cigar-shaped vegetable, is useful chopped and added raw to winter salads. Cooked, it has a slightly bitter flavour which goes particularly well with cheese. This recipe uses the distinctive nutty flavour of chicory to make an unusual dish. It can be served as a separate vegetable course or with meat.

Remove the outer leaves of the chicory and make a cross with a knife at the root. Rinse and boil in salted water until soft. Drain on a cloth and keep hot.

Whip the egg yolks with the cream and stir over a gentle heat until thickened. Add the cayenne pepper and stir in the cheese. Pour over the chicory.

CHICORY AND HAM AU GRATIN

To serve 4:

8 chicory	4 tablespoons of grated
¾ lb/350 g sliced ham	Parmesan cheese
1 pint/60 cl creamy béchamel	2 hard-boiled eggs
sauce (for recipe see page 211)	2 tablespoons of breadcrumbs

Terrine of game (p. 128)

This makes a delicious lunch or supper dish. Remove the outer leaves of the chicory and cross the root with a knife. Boil for ten minutes or until soft. Drain thoroughly and when sufficiently cool to handle wrap a slice of ham securely round each chicory. Put in a deep fireproof dish to keep hot.

Heat the béchamel sauce and add most of the grated cheese, stir well. Pour the sauce over the chicory and add the hard-boiled eggs cut into quarters. Sprinkle on top the breadcrumbs and the rest of the grated cheese. Put in a hot oven or under the grill to brown.

BAKED CAULIFLOWER OMELETTE

Pre-heat oven to 180°C/350°F or gas mark 4
To serve 2:

1 small cauliflower	1 tablespoon of chopped fresh
salted water	parsley
1 onion	4 eggs
1 oz/30 g butter or bacon fat	½ pint/30 cl milk
	salt and pepper

Break cauliflower into sprigs, wash and boil in salted water until cooked but not over-cooked. Cut onion finely and fry gently until golden. Grease a fireproof dish, half an inch (13 mm) in depth, and place the cauliflower in it. Sprinkle onion on the top. Whisk eggs with the milk, add parsley, season and pour over the cauliflower and bake in the oven at 180°C/350°F or gas mark 4 for twenty-five minutes.

SPINACH AND ASPARAGUS IN MOUSSELINE SAUCE

To serve 4–6:

1 lb/500 g fresh or frozen	1 large tin of asparagus tips
spinach	4 egg yolks
salt	

4 tablespoons of asparagus
  juice from the tin
$\frac{1}{4}$ lb/125 g butter

$\frac{1}{2}$ tablespoon of finely-grated
  fresh parsley
grated Parmesan cheese

This dish has all the lightness and brightness of early summer. The tenderness of the vegetables and the frothiness of the sauce recall at once a mild morning in May. In fact, this dish can be constructed at any time of the year with the help of canned and frozen produce – one of the nice things about modern cookery.

If using fresh spinach, wash several times and remove coarse stalks and veins. Put spinach in a saucepan with salt, do not add water. Cover saucepan and place on gentle heat to cook for ten to fifteen minutes. Wrap the spinach leaves round the asparagus tips and place them in bundles in a fireproof dish. Cover with well-buttered greaseproof paper and keep warm at a low temperature.

To make the sauce, put egg yolks in a saucepan and add the asparagus juice. Whisk over a low heat until frothy and add soft butter a little at a time. Keep whisking. When ready, remove the greaseproof paper from the vegetables and pour over the sauce. Sprinkle with a little finely-grated parsley and Parmesan cheese.

Serve either as an accompaniment to a grand dinner or as a dish on its own with small squares of toast.

STUFFED ARTICHOKE HEARTS

To serve 4:

1 × 1 lb/500 g tin of artichoke
  hearts
oil and vinegar dressing
1 tin of sardines

1 tablespoon of mayonnaise
1 tablespoon of grated
  Cheddar cheese
chopped fresh parsley

Place the artichoke hearts on a dish and pour over some oil and vinegar dressing. Remove skin and bones from sardines, mash with a fork, add a tablespoon of mayonnaise and mix to a creamy consistency.

Stuff the artichoke hearts with the sardine cream and sprinkle some grated cheese and parsley on top.

CELERY AND BACON AU GRATIN

To serve 4:

1 × 12 oz/350 g celery hearts	1 teacup of grated cheese
1½ ozs/40 g butter	dash of cayenne pepper
½ pint/30 cl béchamel sauce made with the liquid from the tinned celery	salt and a pinch of sugar
	¼ lb/25 g bacon rashers, cut in strips free of fat and lightly fried

Drain the celery hearts of liquid. Butter a fireproof dish with 1 oz/30 g of the butter and cover the bottom with a little of the béchamel sauce. Cut the celery hearts in half and place them across the dish on top of the sauce. Mix a tablespoon of the cheese into the remaining sauce, add a dash of cayenne pepper and season with salt and a pinch of sugar. Add remaining butter, mix well and cover the celery with the sauce. Sprinkle the remaining cheese on top. Put the dish under a grill or in a hot oven for five or ten minutes. When golden, sprinkle the crisp bacon on top.

OEUFS SUR LE PLAT FLAMENCA

To serve 6:

6 eggs	cayenne pepper
2 lbs/1 Kg tomatoes	1 glass of port
salt and pepper to taste	1 tablespoon of double cream
2 ozs/60 g butter	tomato purée
¼ lb/125 g shrimps	fried bread croûtons

Poach the eggs. Slice tomatoes, season, and fry in butter. When the tomatoes are soft, put through a coarse sieve, add shrimps and bring to the boil. Add a dash of cayenne pepper and the port, simmer, remove from heat and stir in the cream. Pour into a dish two inches deep, dot the tomato purée around and place the poached eggs on top. Arrange the croûtons round the eggs and serve.

BEANS AND BACON

To serve 6:

1 lb/500 g French beans, topped and tailed salt	½ lb/250 g streaky bacon butter

Boil the beans for ten minutes in a covered pan of salted water. Remove carefully with a spoon and tie in bundles like asparagus. Place in a warm, buttered dish. Fry the bacon until golden-brown, cut in strips and sprinkle on the beans.

CELERIAC IN CHEESE SAUCE

To serve 2:

2 celeriac salt	grated cheese ½ pint/30 cl béchamel sauce (for recipe see page 211)

Clean and peel the celeriac. Cut in half and boil in salted water for half an hour. When cooked, scoop out the centres and, adding some grated cheese to the béchamel sauce, pour over the celeriac, replacing the centres. Sprinkle with more grated cheese and put in a hot oven for five minutes.

SWEET PEPPERS WITH RISOTTO FILLING

Pre-heat the oven to 180°C/350°F or gas mark 4
To serve 4:

4 sweet red or green peppers 1 cup of rice, boiled ¼ lb/125 g back bacon, chopped small	1 large onion, chopped 2 ozs/60 g butter ½ lb/250 g chickens' livers, chopped seasoning

Blanch the peppers by bringing them to the boil in salted water. Slice off the tops and remove the seeds. Boil the rice in salted water and gently fry the chopped bacon, chopped chickens' livers and chopped onion in the butter for a few minutes. Fill the peppers with the mixture. Cover with greaseproof paper and cook in the oven set at 180°C/350°F or gas mark 4 for ten minutes.

STUFFED CABBAGE

Pre-heat oven to 180°C/350°F or gas mark 4
To serve 6:

½ lb/250 g minced beef
½ lb/250 g minced pork
½ lb/250 g bread panade (for recipe see page 222)
pepper, salt and a pinch of nutmeg and sugar

½ pint/30 cl milk
1 large cabbage
butter for frying
½ pint/30 cl good beef stock

It seems odd to go back to war-time days to remember an outstanding dish; mostly then, one was at one's wits' end to find sufficient ingredients, let alone create new dishes. For a time during the Second World War, I was with ex-King Peter and ex-Queen Alexandra of Yugoslavia in a house they had in Egham. They were sad days for the King and Queen in exile; they were guarded night and day by security men and were not allowed outside the house at night. Small things mean a lot at times like that and, despite rationing and restrictions, I did my best to cheer them up with my food.

It was on one of these occasions that I first cooked stuffed cabbage, and it turned out to be a great success. King Peter said it reminded him strongly of a Yugoslavian dish whose name I cannot remember, and for an evening everyone forgot their troubles. This dish has, in fact, stood the test of time as there is something in the combination of ingredients which imparts a particularly appetising flavour. The secret, I think, lies in careful handling and a really good beef stock.

Mix the finely-minced meat with the bread panade. Add the eggs and seasoning and stir in the milk. Mix until the consistency resembles sausage meat. Cut the hard part of the stalk out of the cabbage and boil in salted water for fifteen minutes. Separate the leaves and cut out any coarse veins. Fill the leaves with the forcemeat and fold round carefully and put in a fireproof dish. Pour the stock into the frying pan, stir and bring to the boil. Strain the gravy over the cabbage and put the dish in the oven which has been pre-heated to 180°C/350°F or gas mark 4, to cook for half an hour.

TOMATES FARCIE

To serve 5:

1 lb/500 g fresh or frozen peas	pepper
butter	1 sweet red pepper, chopped
2 tablespoons of pickled onions	1 jar of pickled pears, to garnish
10 firm tomatoes	

Boil the peas in salted water for fifteen minutes. Strain and mix in a little butter and the pickled onions. Halve the tomatoes and remove the seeds. Place a small piece of butter inside each half, sprinkle with pepper and fill with the peas and onions. Sprinkle the chopped pepper on top.

This makes a delicious accompaniment to roast beef. Decorate with some small pickled pears.

COCOTTE POTATOES IN TOMATOES

To serve 10:

20 medium-sized tomatoes	2 lbs/1 Kg potatoes, boiled, mashed and creamed
salt and pepper	1 egg, beaten
butter	grated Parmesan cheese

Skin tomatoes and cut in half, remove seeds and sprinkle with salt and pepper. Place a small piece of butter inside each and fill with the creamed potato. Brush the top with beaten egg, sprinkle with cheese and brown under the grill.

JANSSON'S FRESTELSE

Pre-heat oven to 220°C/425°F or gas mark 7
To serve 4:

4 large potatoes
2 ozs/60 g butter
1 large onion
milk

$\frac{1}{4}$ pint/15 cl cream
1 tin anchovies
2 ozs/60 g grated Parmesan or
    Gruyère cheese

This is a favourite supper dish and every Swede worthy of the name has his own variation. We are very fond of our potatoes you see, and are forever devising new ways of cooking them. Jansson's Frestelse are time-honoured and appear even at the grandest parties. Hjördis makes them for her husband, David Niven, and I used to make them for Count Bonde who lived in feudal magnificence at Horningshom Castle in Sweden, surrounded by water, with his own private prison! The Frestelse used to be served at midnight when the Count had his wonderful crayfish parties that went on until the early hours. As a matter of fact, I always associate Jansson's Frestelse with ghosts, because I saw one once at one of these parties when everyone was eating Frestelse very late at night. It was a woman and she walked straight through a wall. It hasn't turned me against Frestelse, though.

Clean the potatoes well. Cut a ring round the top of each potato and bake in the oven. When cooked, cut off the lids and scoop out the inside of the potatoes into a basin and mash up until smooth and free from lumps. Add most of the butter and stir well. Keep hot. Chop the onion finely and boil in a little milk for five minutes. Add the cream to the onion and bring quickly to the boil. Remove at once from the heat and mix with the potato. Half-fill the potato jackets with the mixture, then add a layer of anchovies. Fill with the rest of the potato and top each one with one or two anchovies. Sprinkle the grated cheese on top and dot each potato with a knob of butter. Put the stuffed potatoes on a flat baking sheet in the oven set at 220°C/425°F or gas mark 7 for ten minutes.

BOUCHÉES AUX EPINARD

To serve 6:

½ lb/250 g cooked spinach,
   fresh or frozen
1 oz/30 g butter

salt and sugar, to taste
6 pastry *bouchée* cases

Cook the spinach, sieve and mix in the butter, salt and sugar. Keep pastry cases hot and crisp, and fill them with the cream of spinach just before serving.
   Serve very hot.

BAKED AVOCADO PEAR

Pre-heat oven to 170°C/325°F or gas mark 3
To serve 6 as a first course:

3 avocado pears
¼ pint/15 cl Madeira wine
salt and pepper
1 tablespoon of oil

½ tablespoon of tarragon
   vinegar
½ tablespoon of finely-cut
   chives
finely-chopped fresh parsley

Cut the avocado pears lenghwise in half, remove the stones, place on a baking sheet and fill the halves with the wine. Place in the oven set at 170°C/325°F or gas mark 3, to bake slowly for twenty minutes.
   Mix the seasoning with the oil, vinegar, chives and parsley. Fill the baked pears with the mixture and serve.

ASPARAGUS IN MOUSSELINE SAUCE

To serve 4:

2 bundles of fresh asparagus
   (or tinned)
salt

mousseline sauce (for recipe
   see page 214)

Cut the asparagus tips three inches long. Peel, rinse and tie into four bundles. Boil in salted water for twenty minutes. Remove carefully from the water, drain in a cloth and place in an entrée dish. Remove string and cover with mousseline sauce.

STUFFED ONIONS WITH KIDNEYS AND MUSHROOMS

Pre-heat the oven to 180°C/350°F or gas mark 4
To serve 6:

2 lbs/1 Kg potatoes
$\frac{1}{4}$ pint/15 cl creamy milk
$\frac{1}{4}$ lb/125 g butter
6 large onions
4 lambs' kidneys
$\frac{1}{4}$ lb/125 g mushrooms
salt and pepper to taste

$\frac{1}{2}$ tablespoon of plain flour
$\frac{1}{4}$ pint/15 cl beef stock
$\frac{1}{4}$ pint/15 cl tomato purée
1 tablespoon of sherry
  (optional)
$\frac{1}{4}$ lb/125 g bacon

Cook the potatoes, then mash them and beat in 3 ozs/90 g of the butter and the milk. Peel and rinse the onions, and boil in salted water until soft. Strain and drain on a cloth. Remove the centre of the onions and keep for use in the stuffing.

Cut the kidneys into slices and braise them in a little butter or bacon fat, add the cleaned and sliced mushrooms, and salt and pepper to taste. Stir over a low heat, add the flour and mix well. Pour in the stock and mix. Stir over the heat and bring to the boil, stirring all the while. When thickened, lower the heat and simmer for half an hour with the lid on, stirring once or twice.

When cooked, add the chopped-up onion centres, the tomato purée and the sherry. Bring to the boil slowly and simmer for two minutes. Stuff the onions with this mixture and place them in a flat fireproof dish. Cut the bacon strips and fry until crisp. Strain the bacon fat over the stuffed onions and keep the bacon strips hot. Place the onions in the oven set at 180°C/350°F or gas mark 4 for ten to fifteen minutes.

Spread the creamed potatoes on a serving dish and place the stuffed onions on top. Sprinkle the bacon strips around the dish.

SALADE VERONICA

To serve 4:

1 Cos lettuce
1 tablespoon of tomato purée
juice of a lemon

½ teaspoon of sugar
salt and pepper

Rinse and quarter lettuce, mix the other ingredients together and pour over.

TOMATO AND GREEN PEPPER SALAD

To serve 4:

6 tomatoes
2 tablespoons of chives
1 sweet green pepper, cut in
   strips
French lettuce

1 tablespoon of oil
½ tablespoon of tarragon
   vinegar
salt, pepper and pinch of sugar

Peel tomatoes, cut in quarters, remove the seeds and cut in strips. Chop chives finely. Mix together with pepper strips and serve on a bed of crisp lettuce. Mix the oil, vinegar, salt, pepper and sugar together, and pour over the salad.

BEETROOT SALAD

To serve 4:

1 beetroot
1 cucumber
salt and pepper

equal parts of mayonnaise and
   double cream
lemon juice
lettuce

Cut beetroot into julienne strips and mix with the cucumber, also cut into strips. Add salt and pepper.

Make a mayonnaise sauce from equal parts of mayonnaise and double cream, mixed together with a little lemon juice and salt. Mix into the beetroot and cucumber and serve on a bed of shredded lettuce.

APPLE SALAD

To serve 4:

2 Bramley apples
½ lemon
½ celery heart
2 medium-sized tomatoes
½ lb/250 g Cheddar cheese
¼ lb/125 g Danish blue cheese

½ sweet green pepper
2 tablespoons of mayonnaise
    diluted with 1 tablespoon of
    double cream
dash of cayenne pepper
lettuce

Wash apples and cut them in half across, remove cores and scoop out enough of the flesh to make room for the salad filling. Cut up the scooped-out apple into small pieces and squeeze a little lemon juice over them to keep from discolouring.

Cut up the white part of the celery in small pieces. Skin the tomatoes and cut into sections, remove seeds and cut into strips. Cut the Cheddar cheese into strips and crumble the Danish blue with a fork. Chop up the pepper and mix all the ingredients together with the mayonnaise, adding the cayenne pepper. Fill the apples with the mixture.

Serve the apples on the lettuce.

SALADE CHARLOTTE

To serve 4:

1 French lettuce
1 box of dates
¼ lb/125 g Danish blue cheese

½ sweet red or green pepper
¼ lb/125 g walnuts
1 bunch of grapes

Cut the head of lettuce into four parts, rinse and dry. Stone the dates, cream the cheese and stuff the dates with the cheese. Cut the pepper into

Turkey with walnut stuffing (p.128)
OVERLEAF, LEFT: *Asparagus in mousseline sauce (p. 153)*
OVERLEAF, RIGHT: *vanilla soufflé (p. 165)*

strips, toast the walnuts in the oven and remove the skin. Stone and skin the grapes and arrange the ingredients prettily in a glass bowl.

POTATO SALAD

To serve 4:

4 large potatoes
1 tablespoon of oil
½ tablespoon of vinegar
1 tablespoon of finely-cut chives

salt and sugar to taste
mayonnaise
1 tablespoon of double cream

Boil the potatoes, but do not overcook them. While the potatoes are still quite warm, mix up the oil, vinegar, chives and seasoning and pour over the potatoes. When cooler, mix with mayonnaise and a little cream.

LEGUME SALAD

To serve 4:

1 dessert apple
1 large cooked potato
1 raw celeriac
1 lb/500 g French beans
½ lb/250 g smoked ham

1 tin of mixed carrots and peas
2 onions, cut in thin rings
1 tablespoon of roughly chopped capers (bottled)

For the dressing:
1 tablespoon of nut oil
¼ teaspoon of salt
¼ teaspoon of white pepper

1½ tablespoons of tarragon vinegar

This is a hearty salad, which can be served as a separate course. It is delicious, too, with cold roast beef or steak.

Peel and cut the apple in strips, dice the potato, cut the celeriac in strips, cut the beans, and cut the ham into strips. Mix all together with the carrots, peas and onions. Mix the dressing ingredients together and pour over the salad.

Banana-filled meringues in candied syrup (p. 168)

MOULDED SHRIMP SALAD

To serve 4:

For the aspic:

½ oz/15 g gelatine

¾ pint/40 cl hot water

¼ pint/15 cl white wine or dry sherry

For the salad:

½ lb/250 g frozen shrimps or prawns

1 lettuce, shredded

2 hard-boiled eggs, sliced

2 tomatoes, quartered and skinned

½ cucumber, sliced

watercress, to garnish

Make up the aspic jelly and line a mould when nearly at setting point. Allow to set and arrange half the shrimps or prawns at the bottom. Add a layer of shredded lettuce and sliced eggs, and a further layer of shrimps. Line the side of the mould with the remaining egg slices. Fill the centre with tomatoes and cucumber and cover with the rest of the aspic. Set in the fridge. Turn out on a dish and garnish with watercress.

BUCKLING SALAD

To serve 6:

6 bucklings

3 hard-boiled eggs

2 small beetroots

2 dessert apples

2 boiled potatoes

1 dessertspoon of chopped onion

sliced cucumber and chopped parsley, to garnish

For the dressing:

½ tablespoon of vinegar

½ tablespoon of nut oil

1 tablespoon of tomato purée

1 teaspoon of French mustard

salt, pepper and pinch of sugar

Skin and bone the bucklings and keep in fillets. Chop the whites of the hard-boiled eggs roughly and sieve the yolks. Cut the beetroots, apples and boiled potatoes into cubes. Mix the onion, chopped egg whites, beetroot, apples and potatoes in a basin.

Mix together the salad dressing ingredients and pour over the vegetable salad. Dish up on a flat serving dish and place the buckling on top. Place the sieved egg yolks in a line between the fish. Decorate the buckling fillets with a line of cucumber slices and sprinkle with chopped parsley.

MOULDED MELON SALAD WITH PARMA HAM

To serve 2:

1 honeydew melon	1 packet of pineapple jelly
$\frac{1}{4}$ lb/125 g Parma ham	1 glass of white wine

Cut the melon across, remove seeds and scoop out the fruit carefully with a teaspoon in a series of small egg shapes. Be sure to save the melon juice. Cut the ham in thin strips, mix with the scooped-out melon and return the mixture to the shell. Dissolve the jelly in $\frac{1}{2}$ pint/30 cl of boiling water, add the juice from the melon and enough wine to make up to $\frac{3}{4}$ pint/45 cl. Let it cool until almost at setting point and then pour over the melon salad.

Keep in a cool place.

HOT GRAPEFRUIT SALAD

To serve 6:

3 grapefruit	1 glass of dry white wine
6 teaspoons of caster sugar	dash of cayenne pepper
2 tablespoons of redcurrant jelly	6 black olives
	lettuce, to garnish

Cut grapefruits in half, remove inside skin and seeds and cut into sections. Place on a dish and sprinkle each half with a teaspoon of sugar. Place in a hot oven or under the grill until thoroughly heated.

Melt the redcurrant jelly with wine and a dash of cayenne pepper, bring to the boil and glaze the grapefruit with the mixture. Put a black olive in the centre of each grapefruit half and serve on a lettuce leaf.

SALADE PRINCESSE

To serve 4:

1 tablespoon of oil

2 tablespoons of red wine

1 teaspoon of French mustard

dash of cayenne pepper

salt and sugar

4 bunches watercress (picked over)

Stir oil, wine, mustard and seasoning well together and sprinkle over the watercress.

CUCUMBER SALAD

To serve 4:

1 heart of lettuce

1 cucumber

salt, pepper and sugar to taste

1 tablespoon of white vinegar

1 tablespoon of water

1 tablespoon of chopped fresh parsley

$\frac{1}{2}$ tablespoon of finely-cut chives

Rinse the lettuce, dry and cut in four pieces. Place in the bottom of a salad dish. Peel and cut cucumber into thin slices, sprinkle with salt, pepper and sugar, and put in the middle of the dish. Mix the vinegar, water, parsley and chives together and pour over the cucumber.

VEGETABLE SALAD

To serve 4:

1 lettuce

1 beetroot

2 small leeks

1 tablespoon of water

1 tablespoon of tarragon vinegar

salt, pepper and sugar to taste

Separate the lettuce into leaves. Cut up the beetroot into Julienne strips and cut the white part of the leeks into thin rings. Sprinkle the rings on top of the lettuce and decorate with the beetroot. Mix together the water, vinegar, salt, pepper and sugar and pour over the salad.

AVOCADO PEAR SALAD

To serve 4:

2 avocado pears
$\frac{1}{4}$ pint/15 cl mayonnaise,
    diluted with whipped cream
1 tablespoon of tomato purée
6 ozs/175 g frozen or fresh
    prawns

$\frac{1}{2}$ tablespoon of finely-cut
    chives
salt to taste
chopped red pepper
lemon slices
lettuce hearts

Cut the avocado pears in half lengthwise, remove the stones and scoop out a little of the fruit to make room for the filling. Cut up the fruit and add to the mayonnaise together with the purée, prawns and chives. Add some salt to taste. Fill the pears with the salad and sprinkle the chopped red pepper on top. Garnish with lemon twists.

Serve on a bed of lettuce hearts accompanied by melba toast.

Cakes and Puddings

I USED TO THINK THAT THE SWEET TOOTH WAS BECOMING NEGLECTED. People who spent hours preparing delicious and unusual meat dishes and providing interesting touches to their first courses, would finish the meal rather disappointingly by offering a bit of cheese instead of something sweet.

However, puddings and desserts have become popular once again. Often it is the simple ones that are most in demand. The big draw, for instance, at one of London's smartest restaurants is bread-and-butter pudding. Superbly prepared, of course, but with no frills. And only recently I heard a group of sophisticated young men discussing the best spot to find first-class treacle pudding.

Perhaps my happiest memories of Clarence House are of tea-time in the nursery, during those carefree but numbered days when the Queen was Princess Elizabeth. She would spend the afternoon playing on the lawn with Prince Charles and Princess Anne, carefully folding up the rug and taking in the toys when it was time for tea. Tea was always in the sun-filled nursery, informal and gay with Prince Charles chatting excitedly about the day's events. Even illustrious visitors like foreign kings and queens failed to make it anything but family tea with everyone sharing in the banana sandwiches and sponge cake.

Tea-time with the Queen Mother and Princess Margaret was quite different; they took it at a small table laid with a white cloth in the drawing-room. Then they laid another tablecloth on the floor, on which the dogs were given their meal.

The Royal Family have always been particularly appreciative of sweets and a number of their favourites are included in this chapter.

RICE CROQUETTES WITH PINEAPPLE SAUCE

To serve 4–6:

½ lb/250 g Carolina rice
½ pint/30 cl water
½ pint/30 cl creamy milk
pinch of salt
2 ozs/60 g sugar
2 egg yolks
½ pint/30 cl double cream
1 egg, beaten

2 ozs/60 g breadcrumbs
oil for frying
1 large tin of pineapple rings
1 teaspoon of cornflour
½ pint/30 cl pineapple juice
1 oz/30 g pistachio nuts,
   blanched

This dish was much-liked by Prince Charles when he was still in the nursery.

Boil rice for four minutes in water, add the milk, lower heat and bring slowly to the boil. Add salt and 1 oz/30 g of the sugar. Cover and let the rice simmer slowly until well cooked but the grains are still separate. Remove from heat, mix the egg yolks with two tablespoons of the cream and add to the rice. Mix well and spread on a tray three inches deep to cool. When cold cut into slices with a pastry cutter. Dip the slices first into the beaten egg and then the breadcrumbs and fry in oil until golden-brown. Roll the croquettes in remaining sugar and place a ring of pineapple on top of each one. Keep hot.

To make the sauce, mix the cornflour and pineapple juice over a medium heat and whisk until thick and clear. Glaze the pineapple rings with some sauce and sprinkle pistachio nuts on top.

Serve the rest of the sauce separately with the remaining cream.

PINEAPPLE RICE WITH SABAYON SAUCE

To serve 4–6:

½ lb/250 g Carolina rice
½ pint/30 cl water
½ pint/30 cl milk
1 oz/30 g sugar

pinch of salt
2 egg yolks
½ pint/30 cl double cream
1 fresh pineapple

1 whole egg, beaten

oil

2 ozs/60 g breadcrumbs

caster sugar

For the sauce:

3 fl ozs/8 cl pineapple juice

4 egg yolks

3 fl ozs/8 cl white wine

angelica, for decoration

6 ozs/175 g sugar

Boil rice for four minutes in the water, add the milk, lower the heat and bring slowly back to the boil. Add sugar and salt. Cover and let the rice simmer slowly until well cooked but the grains are still separate. Remove from heat, mix the two egg yolks with two tablespoons of the cream and add to the rice. Mix well.

Cut the top off the fresh pineapple and hollow out the flesh leaving a half-inch thickness round the shell. Save the juice. Cut away the core and cut the rest of the pineapple into small cubes. Mix the fruit with the hot rice and let the mixture cool. When cold, make into pear shapes and dip into the beaten egg and then the breadcrumbs, and fry in oil to a golden colour. Drain on kitchen roll, sprinkle with caster sugar and keep hot.

To make the sauce, put the pineapple juice, wine, sugar and egg yolks all together in a copper or stainless steel saucepan, whisk over a low heat until frothy and thick. Remove from heat and continue to whisk until the sauce is cold. Pour the sauce into the pineapple shell.

Place the pineapple in the centre of a dish and arrange the croquettes around it. Decorate the croquettes with stalks of angelica to resemble pears, and serve with remainder of the cream.

VANILLA SOUFFLÉ

Pre-heat the oven to 190°C/375°F or gas mark 5
To serve 4:

1 vanilla pod or essence to taste

5 eggs

2½ tablespoons of butter

4 egg whites

3 tablespoons of plain flour

a little icing sugar

1 pint/60 cl creamy milk

This smooth, creamy soufflé is fairly easy to make. And once up, it does not go down.

Boil the vanilla pod in the milk, remove from heat, cover the pan and leave until the flavour becomes strong. Alternatively, you can leave out this process and just use vanilla essence. The pod is preferable though.

Melt the butter, add the flour and mix well over a low heat for two or three minutes. Having removed the pod, add the milk a little at a time, and cook, stirring continuously for a further two or three minutes or until the mixture thickens. Pour the mixture into a basin and stir until nearly cold. Whip the whole eggs and sugar together for fifteen minutes and add to the mixture a little at a time, stirring for ten minutes. Lastly, whip egg whites stiffly for ten minutes and fold in gently. Pour into a buttered 2 pint/125 cl soufflé dish and bake in the oven at 190°C/375°F or gas mark 5 for eighteen to twenty minutes. Remove from the oven and dust with icing sugar.

Serve immediately with cream mixed with a little Curaçao or Grand Marnier. Wonderful with fresh strawberries.

PETIT CHOUX SOUFFLÉ AU CARAMEL

Pre-heat oven to 180°C/350°F or gas mark 4
To serve 4–6:

3 tablespoons of golden syrup	grated rind and the juice of 1
2 tablespoons of butter	lemon
5 tablespoons of plain flour	3 tablespoons of caster sugar
$\frac{3}{4}$ pint/40 cl milk	icing sugar
5 eggs, separated	whipped cream

Even at Clarence House the petit choux soufflé was always considered a great treat. It has a delicious lining of oozy caramel, which must be tasted to be believed.

Start by lining a 2 pint/125 cl soufflé dish with caramel which must cool and harden before the rest of the ingredients are added. To make the caramel, bring the golden syrup to the boil over a high heat, stirring to prevent burning, and boil until a dark, moist brown. Watch for burning. Quickly pour the syrup into the soufflé dish and swirl around so that it coats the dish evenly. The caramel should stiffen straight away.

Melt butter in a saucepan, add flour and mix well over a low heat for two minutes. Add the milk and stir until smooth and thick. Simmer slowly for about five minutes or until the mixture thickens and leaves the bottom of the pan. Remove and pour the contents into a basin to cool, stirring all the time. When nearly cold, stir in the beaten egg yolks, lemon juice, rind and the sugar, spoon by spoon. Add these ingredients gradually, stirring continuously for about fifteen minutes.

Beat the egg whites into a stiff froth and continue beating for a further five minutes and fold gently into the mixture. Pour into the caramel-lined soufflé dish and place dish in a baking tin half-filled with water. Bake in the oven at 180°C/350°F or gas mark 4 for forty minutes.

When cooked, dust with icing sugar and serve with whipped cream.

SOUFFLÉ SALTZBURG

Pre-heat oven to 180°C/350°F or gas mark 4
To serve 6 or 8 according to method:

3 ozs/90 g cold butter
5 ozs/150 g caster sugar
½ pint/30 cl double cream
grated rind and juice of
   1 orange

1 tablespoon of Cointreau
5 eggs, separated
icing sugar

Butter a 1 pint/60 cl soufflé dish. Beat egg yolks and sugar until thick, add juice and rind of orange and the Cointreau. Beat egg whites in a separate bowl and when peaked fold into the egg mixture. Pour into the soufflé dish and cook for about twenty-five minutes at 180°C/350°F or gas mark 4 until well risen.

Alternatively, use scooped out oranges (will do about eight oranges): cut off tops of oranges and scoop out flesh leaving the clean pith. Reduce the juice from the flesh in a small pan to about 2 fl oz (6 cl). Grate the discarded orange tops. Make mixture as above and place orange shells in baking tray. Fill to two-thirds with mixture. Cook at 230°C/450°F or gas mark 7 for eight to ten minutes.

BANANES AU CARAMEL

To serve 4:

4 bananas
caster sugar, to coat
2 ozs/60 g butter

½ pint/30 cl double cream,
　whipped
2 tablespoons of golden syrup

Caramel is a most useful and delicious substance in sweet cooking. It is easy to make and a great asset to all sorts of puddings and sweets. It was certainly a great help to me on one occasion at Clarence House when I looked around and found that, due to an oversight, there was no pudding for lunch. The meat course had already gone up and I can remember that there was a certain amount of panic about what to do next. Apart from a few bananas there was nothing much in sight. I reached for the tin of golden syrup and hastily concocted this dish.

Cut the bananas through the middle and then in half. Sprinkle them with caster sugar. Fry gently in butter until they change colour. Cut up, mix with cream and put in individual sundae glasses.

Grease a metal sheet or slab of marble with butter and put the syrup in a frying pan. Melt until dark brown and pour over the greased surface thinly. When hardened, chip with a knife, then sprinkle over the banana cream.

I had a message of appreciation from the royal table for this simple sweet and actually the slightly bitter sweet flavour of the caramel mixed with the creaminess of fried bananas is very attractive. How close the royal table came to being bare, of course, was never disclosed.

BANANA-FILLED MERINGUES IN CANDIED SYRUP

Pre-heat oven to 130°C/250°F or gas mark ½
To serve 6:

3 egg whites
6 level tablespoons of caster
　sugar
½ pint/30 cl double cream

3 bananas
2 ozs/60 g butter
5 tablespoons of golden syrup
juice of 1 lemon

Summer pudding (p. 173)

This is a dish that I have served at many royal dinner parties. It would probably find as much favour as a treat at a children's party.

First, make the meringues overnight. Whip the egg whites until the mixture is stiff enough to enable you to turn the bowl upside down. Whip for a further five minutes. Fold in the six tablespoons of caster sugar. Spoon or pipe the mixture onto a greased and floured baking tray (it will make twelve meringue shells) and put in a very low oven overnight. Alternatively, put in the oven pre-heated to 130°C/250°F or gas mark ½ for one to three hours, or until meringue is firm and dry to the touch. When the meringues have dried out, break each bottom gently with the thumb and turn them up the other way to continue baking.

When the meringues are cooked and cooled, whip up the cream stiffly. Then stick the meringues together with the cream in the usual way, and place on a dish.

Halve and cut the bananas, dip in lemon juice, drain them and sprinkle with a little caster sugar. Fry lightly in butter. When cooled slightly, place on top of the cream between the meringues.

Put the golden syrup in a frying pan and melt until dark brown; be careful of burning. Remove from heat and taking a spoonful at a time, trail haphazardly over the meringues making a spider's web of candied syrup. Two spoons are useful as you can trail the caramel, scraping one against the other. Take care not to touch the caramel with your fingers as it retains its heat.

APPLE SUET PUDDING

To serve 6–8:

Suet pastry (for recipe see page 225)	sugar to taste
	¼ pint/15 cl water
2 lbs/1 Kg Bramley apples	2 or 3 cloves

I once caused rather a stir with apple suet pudding when I served it without warning for Sunday lunch at one of the smart castles in the home counties (not a royal one). "Suet pudding!" said the butler,

Baked Alaska (p. 174)

aghast, as I handed him the dish, "My Lady will never touch it!"

The dish came back scraped clean. I had to keep making it throughout my stay and was later told that I had started a fashion. I had, of course, been making this particular pudding for many years, though mainly I admit, for the nursery.

Grease and line a 2 pint/125 cl pudding basin with suet pastry and let it overlap the rim. Peel, core and cut the apples and mix with sugar. Fill the basin with the apples, pour in the water and place the cloves on top. Fold over paste and cover the basin with greaseproof paper and a cloth.

Place in a steamer with boiling water reaching three-quarters of the way up the basin.

Simmer continuously for four hours on a low heat, taking care that the water does not boil over onto the suet crust or boil dry. Turn out on a dish and sprinkle caster sugar on top.

Serve with cream.

TREACLE PUDDING

To serve 6–8:

5 ozs/150 g golden syrup	8 ozs/250 g plain flour
6 ozs/175 g butter	2 level teaspoons of baking
4 ozs/125 g caster sugar	powder
4 eggs	

Have a steamer ready with boiling water, then grease a 2 pint/125 cl pudding basin with a knob of butter, warm the syrup and add to the basin, swirling it around.

Cream the butter with the sugar, add the eggs one at a time, stirring continuously. Sift the flour with the baking powder and add to the mixture. Fill the basin, cover with greaseproof paper and a pudding cloth.

Place in boiling water in the steamer, the water reaching three-quarters of the way up the basin. Cover the steamer and boil for three-quarters of an hour, adding to the boiling water if necessary. See that the added water is also at boiling point.

Turn out and serve with cream and additional hot syrup if required.

PRINCESS PUDDING

Pre-heat oven to 180°C/350°F or gas mark 4
To serve 6–8:

3 eggs, separated
7 ozs/200 g caster sugar
1 pint/60 cl creamy milk
vanilla essence

8 ozs/250 g fresh breadcrumbs
2 tablespoons of melted
redcurrant jelly
grated rind of 1 lemon

Whisk the yolks of the eggs with 4 ozs/250 g of the sugar. Heat the milk and add to the egg yolks whisking all the time. Add a drop of vanilla essence and the breadcrumbs and allow to stand for fifteen minutes.

Butter a 2 pint/125 cl soufflé dish and fill it with the mixture. Bake in the oven at 180°C/350°F or gas mark 4 for twenty to twenty-five minutes so that it is set but not brown. Spread the top with the melted redcurrant jelly. Whip the egg whites stiff, add the remainder of the sugar and the lemon rind and spread over the pudding. Bake in the oven at 170°C/325°F or gas mark 3 for ten to fifteen minutes till dry and light golden.

APPLE PIE BANBURG

Pre-heat oven to 220°C/425°F or gas mark 7
To serve 4–6:

1 lb/500 g cooking apples
½ lb/250 g sultanas and currants
½ lb/250 g caster sugar
½ teaspoon of cinnamon

juice and grated rind of
1 lemon
short pastry (for recipe see
page 223)

Peel and core the apples and cut in pieces, then add the sultanas and currants and the sugar mixed with cinnamon. Mix them all in a basin and add the juice and rind of the lemon. Fill a 2 pint/125 cl pie dish with the fruit and cover with short pastry. Brush over with milk and sprinkle sugar on top.

Bake for three-quarters of an hour in the oven at 220°C/425°F or gas mark 7.

Serve with cream or vanilla sauce (for recipe, see page 218).

TREACLE TART

Pre-heat oven to 180°C/350°F or gas mark 4
To serve 6:

8 ozs/250 g plain flour	¼ pint/15 cl water
5 ozs/150 g butter	½ lb/250 g golden syrup
1 oz/30 g lard	¼ lb/125 g fresh breadcrumbs
½ oz/15 g caster sugar	1 tablespoon of melted butter
1 egg	

Make the pastry by rubbing the flour with the butter and lard in a basin until crumbly, add the sugar and the lightly beaten egg, and water. It should be fairly stiff. Cover with a cloth and allow to stand in a cold place for half an hour before use. Roll out the pastry to a thickness of a quarter of an inch, and then line a fairly deep baking sheet, approximately ten inches by eight inches.

Put the syrup into the pastry and sprinkle the breadcrumbs on top. Let the tart stand for half an hour. Spread the melted butter on top before placing in the oven. Bake for twenty minutes in the oven at 180°C/350°F or gas mark 4.

Serve with cream.

BREAD AND BUTTER PUDDING

Pre-heat oven to 170°C/325°F or gas mark 3
To serve 6–8:

1 white loaf, medium size	1 pint/60 cl milk
¼ lb/125 g currants	2 tablespoons of caster sugar
¼ lb/125 g sultanas	1 tablespoon of golden syrup
butter	pinch of salt
1 egg, beaten	

Cut loaf into fairly thin slices and remove crust. Rinse the currants and sultanas in hot water to soften. Butter the slices of bread and cut in triangles. Place the bread in a 2 pint/125 cl soufflé dish, layer upon layer, with two tablespoons of dried fruit between the layers. Finish with a layer of bread and butter. Beat the egg, milk, sugar, syrup and salt well together and pour over the bread and butter. Let it soak in for half an hour.

Bake in the oven at 170°C/325°F or gas mark 3 for one hour until the bread comes up, delicately browned on top, like a soufflé.

SUMMER PUDDING

To serve 6–8:

2 lbs/1 Kg redcurrants	sugar to taste
2 lbs/1 Kg raspberries	1 white loaf, medium size

I used to make this dish for the late Lord Rothermere, who liked to have it served on a hot day after a tennis party.

Take half the amount of each fruit and stew in a little water with sugar to taste until soft. Meanwhile, line a 2 pint/125 cl pudding basin with bread slices, about a quarter of an inch thick. Great care must be taken to leave no gaps or the pudding will fall apart. It is really better to double-line the basin, placing the second layer over the seams. Pour the cooked fruit and juice into the pudding and cover the top with a double layer of sliced bread. Put a large plate or saucer over the top so that it is pressing on the bread, and leave overnight with a 1 lb/500 g weight on top.

Sieve the remaining fruit, add caster sugar to taste and mix into a thick purée. Keep cold.

Turn the pudding out and pour the purée on top.

Serve with plain cream or softened ice-cream.

SWEDISH APPLE SPONGE

Pre-heat oven to 180°C/350°F or gas mark 4
To serve 6:

4 ozs/125 g butter	4 ozs/125 g plain flour
4 ozs/125 g sugar	1 teaspoon of baking powder
2 eggs	2 or 3 cooking apples

This is how we bake our sponge puddings in Sweden. It is a very simple process with a particularly pleasant result.

Cream the butter and sugar together, add the eggs, flour and baking powder and put in a 10 inch/25 cm sandwich tin. Peel and cut apples in slices and place them on top of the sponge mixture. Sprinkle with sugar and bake in the oven at 180°C/350°F or gas mark 4, for forty-five minutes or until the sponge shrinks slightly from the sides of the tin.

Serve with vanilla sauce (for recipe see page 218).

BAKED ALASKA

To serve 6–8:

4 egg whites	1 large block of vanilla
8 ozs/250 g caster sugar	ice-cream

Beat egg whites very stiff indeed. Fold in the sugar and beat for a further two minutes. Take the ice-cream straight from the refrigerator, place in a silver (or metal) dish and cover or pipe with the meringue mixture. Put the platter on another tin containing crushed ice and put in a very hot oven for two or three minutes, so that the meringue is just topped with a golden colour.

Serve immediately with fresh fruit such as raspberries or strawberries. Candied syrup is wonderful with this dish if you have time, for the essence of baked Alaska is that it must be cooked and served at a cracking pace.

BROWN BREAD CREAM WITH BLACKCURRANT SAUCE

To serve 4:

¼ pint/15 cl milk	vanilla flavouring, to taste, or a
¼ pint/15 cl double cream	little sherry
2 egg yolks	½ oz/15 g powdered gelatine
3 tablespoons of dry brown	10 ozs/300 g sugar
breadcrumbs	1 lb/500 g fresh blackcurrants

Put the milk, cream and egg yolks in a saucepan and whisk over a gentle heat until mixture reaches the consistency of a thin custard. Add most of the breadcrumbs, the flavouring and the dissolved gelatine and pour into a mould to set. Brown a few breadcrumbs with sugar in the oven and garnish the mould with them.

To make the sauce, pick and rinse the blackcurrants, put through a sieve and mix with the sugar. Serve separately.

CREAM CITRON

To serve 10:

3 or 4 lemons	20 egg yolks
4–6 ozs/125–175 g loaf sugar	macaroons, to decorate
$\frac{3}{4}$ pint/40 cl white wine	

Squeeze the juice of the lemons into a saucepan. Rub the lemon rinds hard with the loaf sugar so that the sugar absorbs the flavour and some particles of the rind, and then put in the saucepan. Add more sugar to taste. Add the wine and the yolks of eggs (yes, twenty). Whisk over a low heat until thickened, but do not boil.

When thick, remove from the heat and whisk until cold. Pour into individual glasses to set. Put little macaroons on top.

CRÈME À LA REINE

To serve 6:

3 egg yolks	$\frac{1}{2}$ oz/15 g gelatine
$\frac{1}{4}$ pint/15 cl milk	$\frac{1}{2}$ pint/30 cl double cream
sugar, to taste	3 oz/75 g bar of nougat
vanilla essence	

Put the egg yolks and milk in a saucepan and whisk over a low heat to thicken. Do not boil. Add some sugar to taste, the vanilla essence and dissolved gelatine. Remove from heat and whisk until cold. When nearly set, whisk the cream to a froth and add to the mixture. Pour into a glass bowl to set.

When set, sprinkle chopped nougat over and serve with hot butter-scotch sauce (for recipe see page 219).

PRUNE PUDDING

Pre-heat oven to 180°C/350°F or gas mark 4
To serve 6:

6 eggs, separated
½ lb/250 g caster sugar
½ pint/30 cl double cream
2 tablespoons of plain flour
¼ lb/125g butter
1 lemon

vanilla essence, to taste
1 lb/250 g tinned or soaked
   prunes
whipping cream
1 oz/30 g chopped almonds

Mix egg yolks and sugar together for fifteen minutes (five minutes if using an electric beater). Add cream, flour and softened butter and whisk over heat until the mixture thickens. Move saucepan from heat and continue whisking until the mixture cools. Add juice of lemon, most of the grated rind and vanilla essence. Then add the beaten egg whites. Lay the prunes (stoned) and a little grated lemon rind on the bottom of a greased fireproof dish, pour mixture on top and bake in the oven at 180°C/350°F or gas mark 4 for one hour. Turn the pudding out on to a dish so that the prunes are uppermost. Serve with whipped cream and sprinkle chopped almonds on top. This pudding can be eaten hot or cold.

BOMBE GLACÉE

To serve 6:

4 egg yolks
2 tablespoons of sugar
½ pint/30 cl milk

½ pint/30 cl double cream
vanilla essence, to taste

Put the egg yolks in a saucepan together with the sugar. Boil the milk separately and add it to the egg mixture, gradually whisking all the time. Keep over a low heat but do not let the mixture boil. Whisk until it thickens like a custard. Remove from heat and whisk until cold. Add vanilla essence to taste. Whisk cream and add to the mixture, pour into an ice tray or bombe mould and put into the freezing compartment of the refrigerator until set.

CRÈME MARRON

To serve 6–8:

1 lb/500 g chestnuts, or tinned chestnut purée
2 ozs/60 g cold butter
4 ozs/125 g caster sugar
1 pint/60 cl double cream, whipped

½ pint/30 cl vanilla ice-cream (optional)
a couple of drops of vanilla essence or maraschino to taste
1 orange

Peel the chestnuts and boil in ¼ pint/15 cl of water until dry and then sieve. Alternatively, you may used tinned chestnut purée. Add the butter and sugar and mix to a smooth cream. Put the mixture in a forcing bag and pipe with a medium fluted nozzle round and round the border of a silver dish, forming folds. Then whip the cream and mix with the vanilla ice-cream. Add the vanilla essence or maraschino, sweeten if necessary. Pile into the centre of the dish. If dispensing with the ice-cream, merely mix the flavouring into the whipped cream. Decorate with peeled and sweetened orange slices.

WHIPPED GOOSEBERRY SNOW

To serve 6–8:

1 packet lime jelly
1 × 14 oz/450 g tin gooseberries

4 egg whites
½ pint/30 cl whipped cream
white grapes, to decorate

Dissolve the lime jelly in ½ pint/30 cl of hot water. Sieve the gooseberries, adding the juice, and mix in with the jelly. Add the beaten egg whites and allow to cool a little. While cooling, whip until frothy. Put into individual glasses. When set, pipe on the whipped cream and decorate with halved white grapes.

BAKED COMICE PEARS

Pre-heat oven to 220°C/425°F or gas mark 7
To serve 6:

6 comice pears
juice of 1 lemon
3 bananas

2 ozs/60 g caster sugar
vanilla ice-cream

Peel the pears, leaving the stalks intact. Rub the surface of the pears with half the lemon juice, then remove cores from the bottom. Mash the bananas with remaining lemon juice and use to stuff the pears. Scratch the pears with a fork vertically. Sprinkle with sugar, place on a baking sheet and put in the oven pre-heated to 220°C/425°F or gas mark 7, for fifteen minutes. Baste once with their own juice to get a glazed effect. Serve hot, round a mound of cold vanilla ice-cream.

GOOD FRUIT SALAD

To serve 8–10:

8 oranges
juice of 1 lemon
1 grapefruit
2 or 3 mandarins or tangerines
2 pears
2 dessert apples

3 bananas
1 bunch of grapes
sugar to taste
maraschino cherries
pistachio nuts

I am always surprised at the different ways in which people make fruit salad. The real point about fruit salad is that every drop of juice from the fruit should be saved and used. This means peeling the fruit over a basin so that not a single drop is wasted. In one establishment where I once worked, the staff were in the habit of throwing away the fruit juice and dressing the salad with a watery sugar syrup.

Squeeze the juice of four oranges and add to the lemon juice in a large bowl. As you cut up the fruit, leave it in the juice to prevent browning.

Peel the other four oranges and free the segments from the skin. Do the same with the grapefruit and mandarins. Peel and core pears, cut into delicate wedges. Peel apples, cut in fairly thick sections and cut across. Pare the bananas into rings. Skin and pip the grapes, leaving as whole as possible. Sprinkle sugar over the fruit and toss.

Decorate with a few maraschino cherries and some pistachio nuts, blanched and skinned.

RASPBERRY FOOL WITH ORANGE CURAÇAO

To serve 6:

2 lbs/1 Kg raspberries, fresh or frozen
sugar to taste

2 tablespoons of orange Curaçao
¾ pint/40 cl double cream
pistachio nuts, to decorate

Sieve the raspberries, add the sugar and orange Curaçao. If using frozen raspberries, defrost but do not add extra sugar. Whip the cream stiff and mix in with the raspberries. Put in individual glasses or fill tartlets. Decorate with pistachio nuts. Serve within one hour.

APRICOT MERINGUE

To serve 6:

1 lb/500 g dried apricots
¾ lb/350 g sugar (for the apricots)
6 egg whites (1 egg white makes two large meringues or three small ones)

12 tablespoons of sugar
whipped cream
1 teaspoon of orange Curaçao (optional)

Soak the apricots overnight. Cover with water, bring to the boil and simmer until cooked. Sieve with a nylon sieve, put back in saucepan, add sugar and mash with a fork. Never add sugar in the cooking stage as most of it is wasted when the fruit is sieved. Put the apricots in a glass dish to cool, adding more sugar if required.

Make the meringues overnight according to the following method. First, see that all the utensils, bowl, beaters etc., are scrupulously clean and free from any trace of grease. Whip the egg whites until the mixture is stiff enough to enable you to turn the bowl upside down without disaster, then fold in the sugar. Spoon the mixture onto a greased and floured baking tray and put in a very, very low oven overnight. The meringues should turn a delicate pink in colour; never brown which means they have been cooked at too high a temperature. Alternatively, you can put the mixture into the oven set at 130°C/250°F or gas mark ½, for one to three hours, or until the meringues are firm and dry to the touch. When the meringues have dried out, break the bottom gently with your thumb and turn them over so that they dry out in the middle.

Whip up the cream and orange Curaçao (optional) and stick the meringues together round the dish containing the apricot purée.

There can be no hitch with this dish; the apricots can be puréed the day before and the meringues ready for you on the morning of the day they are needed. Keep in a cool larder.

MUSCAT GRAPES EN GELÉE

To serve 6–8:

1 packet of orange jelly	2 egg whites
½ pint/30 cl boiling water	whipped cream
½ pint/30 cl white wine	1 orange
1 lb/500 g Muscat grapes	pistachio nuts

Dissolve the jelly in the hot water, add the wine and cool. Skin and stone the grapes and put them in individual glasses, leaving aside a few for decoration. When the jelly is nearly set, whip it to a froth, add two beaten egg whites and fill the glasses. Leave to set and decorate with piped whipped cream, the orange cut in sections, and the rest of the grapes. Sprinkle pistachio nuts on top.

SWEET PANCAKES

To make about 12 pancakes:

3 eggs	½ tablespoon of caster sugar
4 ozs/125 g plain flour	pinch of salt

Crème à la reine (p. 175)
OVERLEAF, LEFT: *Crème marron (p. 177)*
OVERLEAF, RIGHT: *Baked comice pears (p. 178)*

½ pint/30 cl milk
¼ pint/15 cl cold water

¼ pint/15 cl double cream
unsalted butter

Beat the eggs with the water. Sift the flour, sugar and salt and add to the beaten egg. Mix well to a smooth paste. Then add the milk and cream. Allow the mixture to stand for half an hour.

Put a teaspoon of unsalted butter in a crêpe pan and melt until frothing. Add a ladle full of batter to coat crêpe pan and fry for two minutes until golden-brown on the bottom. Then turn pancake over and fry until golden-brown on reverse side. Fill with a soufflé mixture or ice-cream and serve immediately.

CRÈME À LA DUCHESSE

To serve 6:

½ pint/30 cl milk
½ pint/30 cl double cream
6 eggs, separated
12 tablespoons of caster sugar
grated rind of 1 orange and 1
   lemon

a few drops of vanilla or
   Curaçao
almond flakes or pistachio
   nuts, to decorate

Boil the milk and the cream together. Whisk the egg whites to a stiff froth. Add the sugar, a little at a time, and then the orange and lemon rind. Using a tablespoon, drop balls of the egg mixture into the simmering milk. The meringues will puff up to three times their original size and should be turned briefly during cooking. When set, remove carefully with a draining spoon and put into a sieve to drain thoroughly.

Put four yolks of eggs into another saucepan and add a little vanilla or Curaçao to taste. Whisk well and add the hot milk, whisking all the time over a low heat. Do not boil. Continue whisking until thickened. Remove from heat and carry on whisking until cold. Pour into a glass dish and then float the meringue balls on top.

Sprinkle with toasted almond flakes or chopped pistachio nuts.

Serve cold with strawberry sauce (for recipe see page 218).

Good fruit salad (p. 178)

CRÊPES SUZETTE À LA SUÉDOISE

To make 12 crêpes:

3 eggs

$\frac{1}{4}$ pint/15 cl water

1 teaspoon of sugar

$\frac{1}{2}$ teaspoon of salt

3 ozs/90 g plain flour

$\frac{1}{4}$ pint/15 cl double cream

2 tablespoons of nut oil

For the sauce:

$\frac{1}{2}$ pint/30 cl double cream

2 tablespoons of caster sugar

rind and juice of 1 orange

a few drops of vanilla

2 tablespoons of orange
    Curaçao

lemon juice

Beat the eggs with water, add the sugar, salt and flour. Mix until very smooth, add the cream and mix well. Let the mixture rest for thirty minutes.

To cook the crêpes, have the pan greased with just enough oil so that the batter will not stick. Drop one tablespoon of the batter at a time into the heated pan and tip so that the mixture spreads as thinly as possible. Cook until golden-brown on each side. Repeat the process until all the batter is used up, fold the pancakes in quarters and stack one on top of another in a warm but not hot oven.

To make the sauce, bring cream and sugar to the boil, add orange juice, rind and vanilla essence. Boil for two minutes and then add the Curaçao slowly.

Serve pancakes by squeezing a little lemon juice over them, then sprinkle a little caster sugar on top and put under the grill for a minute to brown.

Serve the hot sauce separately.

MELON SURPRISE

To serve 4:

1 large melon

1 lb/500 g fresh or frozen
    strawberries

$\frac{1}{4}$ lb/125 g sugar

3 bananas

juice of $\frac{1}{2}$ a lemon

crushed ice

cream

Cut the top off the melon, remove seeds, scoop out the fruit and cut into cubes. Sieve the strawberries and blend into the melon cubes, cut bananas into slices and toss in lemon juice. Add sugar to taste. Mix all together and fill the melon shell with the mixture.

Replace the lid and make very cold.

Serve on crushed ice, with cream.

PEACH MERINGUE WITH VANILLA CREAM

Pre-heat oven to 170°C/325°F or gas mark 3
To serve 6:

6 small round sponge cakes
1 tin of California peaches
1 tablespoon of Grand Marnier
3 tablespoons of double cream
4 egg whites

6 tablespoons of caster sugar
1 oz/30 g icing sugar
1 pint/60 cl vanilla sauce (for recipe, see page 218)

Place the sponge cakes on a dish and put half a peach on each cake. Mix the Grand Marnier with the cream and spread on the cakes. Whip egg whites into a stiff froth, add sugar and pipe over the dish. Place in the oven pre-heated to 170°C/325°F or gas mark 3 until the meringue turns a very light brown.

Sprinkle with icing sugar and serve with vanilla sauce.

POIRES MARASCHINO AUX ANANAS

To serve 6:

1 pint/60 cl water
6 ozs/175 g caster sugar
juice of 1 lemon
6 large comice pears
2 slices of lemon

1 × 14 oz/450 g tin of pineapple rings or 1 small pineapple
6 fl ozs/20 cl maraschino
angelica, to decorate

Boil the water, sugar and lemon juice together to make a syrup. Peel pears and remove cores carefully leaving the pears intact. Drop the pears into the boiling syrup with the lemon slices. Boil for five minutes, remove from heat and let them cool in the syrup.

If using fresh pineapple, cut the slices half an inch thick and remove the core. Cut off skin with a corrugated cutting ring. Drop the pineapple rings in the syrup with the pears and leave until cold. Pour over $\frac{1}{4}$ pint/15 cl of maraschino.

Stand the pears upright on a flat crystal dish and place the pineapple rings on top of the pears like hats. Cut the stalk from the angelica and fix on top of each pear, so that it shows through the pineapple ring.

Serve with whipped cream flavoured with the rest of the maraschino.

GLACÉ SOUFFLÉ GRAND MARNIER

To serve 6–8:

6 ozs/175 g sugar	$\frac{1}{2}$ teaspoon of vanilla essence
$\frac{1}{4}$ pint/15 cl water	$1\frac{1}{4}$ pints/75 cl double cream
8 egg yolks	oil
$\frac{1}{4}$ pint/15 cl Grand Marnier	

When cooking for the Queen Mother at Clarence House, I soon discovered that she was very appreciative of good home-made ice-cream. I was very happy indeed when I received kind messages for my efforts and I was soon spurred on to try new variations. This is a light and charming dish for a summer's day.

Boil the sugar and water together for one minute and then remove from heat. Whisk and allow to cool a little. Add the egg yolks, one at a time, whisking continuously over a gentle heat. Do not boil. Once the mixture is very thick, remove from heat and whisk until cold. When cold, add the Grand Marnier and the vanilla essence. Whip the cream and stir into the egg mixture. Line a soufflé dish with greaseproof paper brushed with oil and fill the dish with the parfait mixture.

Freeze for four to five hours in a freezer or the freezing compartment of a refrigerator. Remove fifteen minutes before serving. Turn out on a dish, remove the paper and serve with sieved fresh strawberry sauce (for recipe see page 218) and biscuits.

GINGER SPONGE CAKE

Pre-heat oven to 190°C/375°F or gas mark 5
To make 1 × two-layer 8-inch/20-cm cake:

2 ozs/60 g butter
4 ozs/125 g sugar
2½ ozs/75 g golden syrup
2½ ozs/75 g black treacle
¼ pint/15 cl milk
1 egg, well beaten

6 ozs/175 g self-raising flour
1 teaspoon of cinnamon
1 teaspoon of ground ginger
¼ teaspoon of ground cloves
½ teaspoon of bicarbonate of
   soda

For the filling:
2 dessertspoons of butter
½ lb/250 g icing sugar

a few drops of hot water and
   vanilla essence, mixed

Beat butter and sugar to a cream, add the syrup, treacle, milk and egg. Sieve the flour, cinnamon, ginger, cloves and bicarbonate of soda into the mixture. Divide the mixture into two sandwich tins lined with greased paper. Bake in the oven at 190°C/375°F or gas mark 5 for twenty minutes, or until a skewer comes out clean. Allow to cool.

To make the filling, mix together all the ingredients and spread between the sandwich halves.

CURRANT CAKE

Pre-heat oven to 140°C/275°F or gas mark 1
To make 1 × 9-inch/22-cm cake:

¾ lb/350 g self-raising flour
½ lb/250 g butter
½ lb/250 g sugar
1¼ lbs/600 g currants, cleaned
   and dried

¼ lb/125 g almonds, blanched
   and finely chopped
milk
3 eggs, beaten
1 tablespoon of brandy

Put the flour in a basin and rub the butter into the flour. Mix in the sugar, currants and the almonds. Mix a little milk with the beaten eggs. Add the brandy and mix with all the other ingredients. Bake in the oven at 140°C/275°F or gas mark 1 for two hours.

MADEIRA CAKE

Pre-heat oven to 180°C/350°F or gas mark 4
To make 1 × 10-inch/25-cm cake

6½ ozs/185 g butter
6½ ozs/185 g sugar
6 eggs
12 ozs/350 g plain flour

¼ pint/15 cl single cream
2 teaspoons of baking powder
candied peel

Cream the butter and the sugar together, whisk in the eggs one by one with a tablespoon of flour for each egg. Add the cream and mix in the baking powder, sieved, with the remaining flour.

Put the mixture in a greased and floured baking tin, place some slices of candied peel on top of the mixture. Bake in the oven at 180°C/350°F or gas mark 4 for one hour and twenty minutes.

SPONGE SANDWICH CAKE

Pre-heat oven to 220°C/425°F or gas mark 7
To make 1× two-layer 8-inch/20-cm cake:

4 eggs
½ lb/250 g caster sugar
3 ozs/90 g plain flour
2 ozs/60 g potato or cornflour

2 teaspoons of baking powder
¼ pint/15 cl whipped cream
jam
icing sugar

Break the eggs into a bowl, whisk lightly and add the sugar. Whisk for twenty minutes (ten minutes if you are using an electric whisk). Sieve the flour and potato or cornflour with the baking powder and add to the mixture. Mix well and pour into two buttered and floured sandwich tins. Bake on the middle shelf of the oven at 220°C/425°F or gas mark 7 for twenty-five minutes.

When cool, sandwich the cakes together with the cream and jam, and dust the top with sieved icing sugar.

CHOCOLATE AND COFFEE CAKE

Pre-heat oven to 170°C/325°F or gas mark 3
To make × 8-inch/20-cm cake:

8 ozs/250 g butter
8 ozs/250 g caster sugar
5 eggs, separated
1 tablespoon of orange
   marmalade

6 ozs/175 g cooking chocolate
8 ozs/250 g plain flour
2 teaspoons of baking powder
2 ozs/60 g ground sweet
   almonds

For the filling:
4 ozs/125 g butter
8 ozs/250 g icing sugar

2 tablespoons of coffee
   essence, or instant coffee
   mixed with 2 tablespoons of
   warm water

This was my most popular cake with the Royal Family, made to my own recipe. Everyone seemed to like it and it went everywhere. By special request I have sent it off to Windsor, Balmoral and Sandringham, and the Queen Mother would request it for her birthday.

Beat butter and sugar to a light cream. Add egg yolks and marmalade. Stir in the melted chocolate. Add flour, baking powder and almonds. Whip egg whites stiff and fold in lightly. Pour into a greased cake tin and bake in the oven at 170°C/325°F or gas mark 3 for one hour and fifteen minutes. When cool, cut in half.

To make the filling, cream together all the ingredients and warm slightly before spreading on the sandwich halves and the top of the cake.

CHILDREN'S BIRTHDAY CAKE

Pre-heat oven to 200°C/400°F or gas mark 6
To make 1 × 9-inch/22-cm cake:

8 eggs
1 lb/500 g caster sugar
4 teaspoons of baking powder
6 ozs/175 g plain flour

4 ozs/125 g cornflour
redcurrant jelly
½ pint/30 cl whipped cream

For the icing:

20 ozs/600 g icing sugar   1 egg white
1 dessertspoon of water   colouring, if desired

Break the eggs into a basin, add the sugar and mix for fifteen to twenty minutes (ten minutes if you are using an electric whisk). Add the baking powder to the flour and sieve into the mixture. Mix well and fill a large cake tin lined with greased paper, and bake in the oven at 200°C/400°F or gas mark 6 for three-quarters of an hour. Remove from oven and cool on a wire tray. When cold, cut the cake in three layers. Spread one layer with redcurrant jelly and the other with cream.

To make the icing, mix together all the ingredients until thick and smooth. Beat until the mixture holds a peak. Cover the cake with the mixture, using a palette knife dipped frequently in boiling water and shaken dry.

CHEESE CAKES

Pre-heat oven to 180°C/350°F or gas mark 4
To make 8–10 cheese cakes:

$\frac{1}{4}$ lb/125 g Cheshire cheese,   salt and pinch of cayenne
    finely grated   pepper
$\frac{1}{4}$ lb/125 g Parmesan cheese,   2 egg yolks
    grated   1 egg white
$\frac{1}{4}$ lb/125 g plain flour   cream cheese

Catering for savoury tastes at a children's party, you will find these cheese cakes popular. Good for grown-ups too.

Mix together the Cheshire cheese, Parmesan cheese, flour, salt, pepper and the egg yolks. Roll out and cut into round cakes a quarter of an inch thick with a pastry cutter. Brush with the egg white mixed with a little water. Bake in the oven at 180°C/350°F or gas mark 4, until golden-brown. When cold, make sandwiches of the cakes filled with cream cheese.

FUDGE TOFFEE

To make 1 lb/500 g of toffee:

2 ozs/60 g butter $\frac{1}{4}$ pint/15 cl condensed milk
1 lb/500 g demerara sugar   vanilla flavouring

Some extra special fudge toffee is always popular for handing round at a children's party. It might also be an occasion for the young host or hostess to make their first attempt at cooking.

Melt the butter in a saucepan over a low heat, add the sugar and bring to the boil, stirring all the time. Then add the condensed milk mixed with 2 tablespoons of water. Stir and simmer for about twenty-five minutes. Remove from the heat and add a few drops of vanilla. Grease a baking sheet with butter and pour on the toffee to cool. Before it cools completely, mark with a knife into squares which can be separated when cold.

CHILEAN BUNS

Pre-heat oven to 220°C/425°F or gas mark 7
To make 8 small buns:

6 ozs/175 g plain flour $\frac{1}{2}$ teaspoon of salt
1 tablespoon of butter $\frac{1}{4}$ pint/15 cl milk
1 teaspoon of baking powder

Here are some light buns suitable for a children's tea. I call them Chilean buns because I was given the recipe by the Chilean Embassy after a member of the Royal Family had enjoyed them there for tea.

Mix all the ingredients together into a hard dough and roll into a long sausage. Cut into small bun shapes, place on a greased baking sheet and cross them with the back of a knife. Place in the oven which has been pre-heated to 220°C/425°F or gas mark 7, for five to ten minutes.

APPLE MERINGUE SPONGE

Pre-heat oven to 230°C/450°F or gas mark 8
To make 1 × two-layer 8-inch/20-cm cake:

For the sponge:

4 eggs

equal weight of the eggs in
  caster sugar

half the weight of the eggs in
  plain flour

For the filling:

4 cooking apples

sugar to taste

juice of ½ lemon

¼ pint/15 cl single cream

½ teaspoon of vanilla essence

For the meringue:

3 egg whites

3 tablespoons of caster sugar

grated rind of ½ a lemon

This is an apple meringue sponge with a difference. The difference, I think, lies mainly in the lightness of the sponge and the cream filling which flavours the cake if left to soak overnight.

To make the sponge, whip the whole eggs and sugar together for twenty-five minutes with a whisk or ten minutes with electric beaters. Mix the flour, cornflour and baking powder together and sieve, mix with the sugar and eggs. Put onto two flat, greased tins and bake in the oven at 220°C/425°F or gas mark 7 for twenty minutes. Remove and turn out, and when cold place in a flat fireproof dish.

Peel and core the apples, cut into thin slices and poach with a little sugar and squeeze of lemon until tender. Drain. Mix cream with vanilla essence and spread over each cake. Arrange slices of apple on top of one of the cakes and place other on top as a lid.

Whip up the egg whites and then fold in the sugar and the lemon rind. Pile it up on top of the apple and place in a very hot oven (230°C/450°F or gas mark 8) for two minutes or until tips of peaks are golden-brown. Serve immediately.

MRS MCKEE'S CHRISTMAS CAKE

Pre-heat oven to 150°C/300°F or gas mark 2
To make 1 × 12-inch/30-cm cake:

1 lb/500 g butter
1 lb/500 g caster sugar
2 tablespoons of orange
    marmalade
1 tablespoon of black treacle
10 eggs, separated
1½ lbs/750 g plain flour
1 lb/500 g currants

1 lb/500 g sultanas
½ lb/250 g stoned raisins
¼ lb/125 g candied peel
½ teaspoon of nutmeg
pinch of salt
1 teaspoon of vanilla essence
½ teaspoon of almond essence
2 tablespoons of rum

If you like dark, stodgy Christmas cake, this recipe is not for you. This cake is lighter in appearance and texture than the traditional kind but will keep equally well for a year or more. It is the cake that the Royal Family enjoyed. I would bake it on the 13th of November when all the royal puddings were prepared, keep it and send it off to Sandringham for Christmas Day.

Stir butter and sugar together until creamy. Add marmalade and treacle. Drop in the egg yolks one at a time and a tablespoon of flour to each yolk, stirring continuously. Mix all the fruit in with the flour. Add nutmeg and pinch of salt, the essences and the rum. Beat the egg whites to a stiff snow and fold in.

Line a tin with paper, grease it well, fill it with the mixture and bake in the oven at 150°C/300°F or gas mark 2 for two to three hours.

PINEAPPLE CAKE

Pre-heat oven to 180°C/350°F or gas mark 4
To make 1 × 9-inch/22-cm cake:

1 fresh pineapple or 1 large tin
    of pineapple rings
8 ozs/250 g sugar
8 ozs/250 g butter
3 eggs

6 ozs/175 plain flour
2 ozs/60 g cornflour
1 heaped teaspoon of baking
    powder

Pulp the fresh or tinned pineapple by grating or putting in a mixer. Add just a little of the sugar to taste. Put in a greased fireproof dish and keep warm. Cream together the butter, sugar, eggs, flour, cornflour and baking powder. Put the cake mixture on top of the pineapple pulp and bake in the oven at 180°C/350°F or gas mark 4 for three-quarters of an hour. Loosen carefully. Turn out and serve with cream.

ALMOND BISCUITS

Pre-heat oven to 220°C/425°F or gas mark 7
To serve 6:

½ lb/250 g unblanched almonds   butter
2 egg whites   plain flour
4 tablespoons of caster sugar

Chop the almonds roughly. Whip whites of egg with the sugar for two or three minutes and add the almonds.

Spread on a well-buttered and floured tin and bake in the oven at 220°C/425°F or gas mark 7 for five to seven minutes or until light brown. When ready, remove, cool a little and cut while still warm into sections four inches long and two inches wide. Return to the oven to heat and then quickly remove the biscuits with a knife. Bend them, while still warm, over a rolling pin. Leave to cool and become crispy.

Crème à la duchesse (p. 181)

Special Occasions

IN THIS COUNTRY MOST OF THE OCCASIONS THAT PEOPLE RATE AS special seem to have some connection with sport. This is quite logical, of course, since healthy exercise produces healthy appetites. There may, too, be feelings of guilt that one should not really be indulging oneself unless a lot of hard work has been put in beforehand. I can't help thinking, for instance, that the thunderous exercise that takes place in the hunting season, also has something to do with the wild abandon that goes on at some hunt balls and horse show festivities. One cannot exactly say that the tennis parties in English country gardens are the scene of mad revels, but the China tea and cucumber sandwiches doubtless taste all the better for a bit of activity.

At any rate, to my mind, all these sporting occasions compare quite favourably with the sterility of so many London cocktail parties, where the chief purpose seems to be to deaden palate, appetite and senses.

I have chosen the recipes in this chapter to go with a particular type of sport, but they will, of course, go equally well with any number of different activities.

THE SHOOTING LUNCH

lobster salad   *curried eggs*

cold minced veal cutlets
roast lamb cutlets in aspic with glazed onions

potato salad   *tomato and pepper salad*

apple turnovers
cheese selection

Poires maraschino aux ananas (p. 183)

LOBSTER SALAD

To serve 4:

1 large cooked lobster	salt and cayenne pepper to
¼ pint/15 cl double cream	taste
½ pint/30 cl mayonnaise	cucumber slices and chopped
juice of ½ lemon	fresh parsley, to garnish

Cut the lobster in half lengthways and remove the meat. Save the red coral part of the lobster and the green creamy bit inside. Break the claws and remove the meat. Cut the lobster meat into large pieces. Sieve the red coral and keep for decoration. Mix in the greenish cream with the lobster meat in a bowl. Whip the cream to a froth and add to the mayonnaise, together with the lemon juice, salt and cayenne pepper. Mix half of the mayonnaise mixture with the lobster. Put the lobster in a dish on a bed of lettuce and cover with the rest of the mayonnaise. Garnish with the sieved red coral in a pattern on top and slices of unpeeled cucumber. Sprinkle chopped parsley over the cucumber.

CURRIED EGGS

To make up to 12 eggs:

1 large onion	dash of paprika
1 apple	1 pint/60 cl hot chicken stock
2 ozs/60 g butter	1 tablespoon of sultanas
2 tablespoons of plain flour	1 tablespoon of grated coconut
2 tablespoons of curry powder	3 fl ozs/8 cl double cream
1 tablespoon of Escoffier	juice of ½ lemon
chutney	2 hard-boiled eggs per person
1 tablespoon of Worcester	mustard and cress
sauce	¼ lb/125 g patna rice

Peel and chop the onion, core and chop the apple. Melt the butter in a saucepan, add the onion and braise gently to a golden colour. Add the flour and curry powder and stir well. Add the apple, chutney, Worcester sauce and paprika. Pour in the hot stock and mix well. Lastly, add the sultanas and coconut and bring to the boil. Cook for twenty minutes. Strain and add the cream and the lemon juice. Cover the eggs with the sauce.

Allow to cool and garnish with mustard and cress. Boil rice in salted water and serve with the curried eggs.

COLD MINCED VEAL CUTLETS

To serve 6–8:

1 lb/500 g minced veal	salt and pepper to taste
1 lb/500 g bread panade (for recipe, see page 222)	½ pint/30 cl creamy milk
1 egg	1 teaspoon of sugar
	butter

Mix the veal and bread panade in a bowl. Stir in the egg and the seasoning. Add the milk gradually and stir for five or ten minutes. Add the sugar and mix well. Shape into half-inch thick cutlets and fry in butter until golden-brown on both sides. When fried put in a baking tin with a few knobs of butter and place in a hot oven for ten minutes.

Allow to cool.

ROAST LAMB CUTLETS IN ASPIC WITH GLAZED ONIONS

Pre-heat oven to 220°C/425°F or gas mark 7
To serve 6–8:

3 lbs/1.5 Kg best end of neck of lamb	½ pint/30 cl good stock
salt and pepper	1 teaspoon of Bovril
1 clove of garlic, sliced	dash of Worcester sauce
	1 pint/60 cl aspic

For the glazed onions:

12 button onions	a knob of butter
1 tablespoon of tomato sauce	1 teaspoon of sugar

See that the backbone is chined and trim off unwanted fat. Trim the end of the bones of meat and fat, up to about an inch. Rub in some salt and pepper and insert small pieces of garlic. Roast in the oven at 220°C/425°F or gas mark 4 for one hour, basting frequently. When cooked, place the meat on a dish and remove the garlic. Drain off all the fat from the gravy and stir in the stock. Add the Bovril and a dash of Worcester sauce and bring to the boil over a brisk heat. Reduce to a glazed sauce. Strain and cover the meat with the sauce.

When the meat is cold, divide into cutlets and cover with aspic.

To make the glazed onions, peel then cook the onions in salted water until soft. Strain and add one tablespoon of tomato sauce, a knob of butter and one teaspoon of sugar. Boil down to a glaze and pour over the onions. When cool, place in the dish with the lamb cutlets.

POTATO SALAD
(For recipe, see page 157)

TOMATO AND GREEN PEPPER SALAD
(For recipe, see page 155)

APPLE TURNOVERS

Pre-heat oven to 220°C/425°F or gas mark 4
to make 18–20:

1 lb/500 g puff pastry (for recipe, see page 224)	icing sugar ½ pint/30 cl thick apple purée

Make the puff pastry according to the method on page 224. Roll out a quarter of an inch thick and cut out rounds about four inches across with a fancy pastry cutter. Place some thick apple purée in the middle of the pastry rounds. Moisten the edges of the pastry with a little water. Fold over to a half circle and press the edges together.

Place on a baking sheet and bake in the oven at 220°C/425°F or gas mark 4 for fifteen minutes, then lower the heat and bake for another five or ten minutes. When ready, dust some icing sugar on top.

Jam or fruit of any kind can be used instead of the apple purée.

CHEESE SELECTION

Boursin − a very pleasant French dessert cheese
Chantilly − delicious with fruit
Port Salut − mild and pleasing
Swedish Herrgurds Ost − mild, but sharp when ripe

* * *

THE TENNIS PARTY

cucumber sandwiches
biscuit crunchies with ice-cream   *gooey chocolate cake*
iced tea   *iced coffee*

CUCUMBER SANDWICHES

It is most important that the bread and cucumber are very thinly sliced.
Add a sprinkling of salt and a drop of tarragon vinegar to each
sandwich.

BISCUIT CRUNCHIES

Pre-heat oven to 180°C/350°F or gas mark 4
To make 18–20 biscuits:

$\frac{1}{4}$ lb/125 g butter   2 teaspoons of ground ginger
2 ozs/60 g sugar   2 egg whites
$2\frac{1}{2}$ ozs/75 g plain flour

Beat butter and sugar until fluffy. Mix the flour and ginger together and
add to the mixture. Whip egg whites until stiff. Fold in carefully. Shape
into slabs, three inches wide by four inches, and place on a greased tin.
Bake in the oven at 180°C/350°F or gas mark 4 until lightly browned.
Remove and roll up lightly.

Serve with ice-cream.

GOOEY CHOCOLATE CAKE

Pre-heat oven to 150°C/300°F or gas mark 2
To make 1 × 8-inch/20-cm cake:

8 ozs/250 g butter
8 ozs/250 g sugar
5 eggs, separated
1 tablespoon of orange
  marmalade

5 ozs/150 g cooking chocolate
8 ozs/250 g plain flour
2 teaspoons of baking powder
2 ozs/60 g ground sweet
  almonds

For the chocolate butter icing:
¼ lb/125 g unsweetened plain
  chocolate
½ lb/250 g icing sugar
4 ozs/125 g butter, softened

1 egg, beaten
a few drops of vanilla and
  almond essence

Beat the butter and sugar to a light cream. Add the egg yolks and marmalade. Stir in the chocolate, previously melted over a low heat. Add the flour, baking powder and almonds. Whip egg whites and fold in lightly. Pour into a greased tin and bake in the oven at 150°C/300°F or gas mark 2, for one hour and fifteen minutes.

When cool, cut into three layers.

To make the icing, melt the chocolate over a low heat. Sieve the icing sugar into a bowl, stir in the soft butter, add the chocolate and beaten egg and stir until smooth and light. Add the flavouring and spread immediately between the layers of chocolate cake and on the top with a palette knife. Some of the icing can be piped on top with a forcing bag.

ICED TEA

2 teaspoons of China tea (Earl
  Grey)
2 teaspoons of Indian tea
1½ pints/90 cl boiling water

½ pint/30 cl fresh orange juice,
  strained
juice of 1 lemon, strained
demerara sugar, to taste
ice

Make the tea in the usual way and brew for five to eight minutes. Strain and add the orange and lemon juice. Add demerara sugar (or serve separately). Allow to cool in tall glasses with ice.

ICED COFFEE

1½ ozs/40 g good-quality coffee   1 block of vanilla ice-cream
1 pint/60 cl boiling water

Place the coffee in a percolater and add the boiling water at intervals. Keep the pot hot but do not boil. Leave to cool. When cold, pour into tall glasses and scoop a tablespoon of ice-cream into each one.

*   *   *

THE HUNTING BREAKFAST

fruit and vegetable juices
cold ham
egg, bacon, sausages, mushrooms
fried egg balls (morning only treat)
toast, marmalade, honey
coffee and cream

Catering for a hunting party is ideally simple. You send the guests out with a big, hearty breakfast under their belts, with perhaps one treat. They are then gone for the rest of the day when the time is your own. On their return, give them more breakfast – without the morning treat, but with whisky.

COLD HAM

1 ham or gammon, size
   according to numbers
a couple of wisps of hay
2 teaspoons of mustard
   powder

a little beer
2 tablespoons of demerara
   sugar
1 teaspoon of ground
   cinnamon

Soak the ham for twenty-four hours. Scrub and wash with water. Place in a big saucepan and cover with water. Bring to the boil and add the wisps of hay. Cover and simmer at the rate of twenty-five minutes to the pound (500 g). When cooked, remove the pan from the heat, turn the ham upside down and leave to cool in its own juice. Remove the skin and any surplus fat. Put in a roasting tin.

Mix the mustard powder with a little beer and spread evenly over the ham. Mix the demerara sugar with the cinnamon and press firmly into the ham. Place in a hot oven to glaze for a few minutes. Remove and allow to cool before serving.

FRIED EGG BALLS

4 hard-boiled eggs	plain flour
½ pint/30 cl thick English butter sauce (for recipe, see page 217)	egg breadcrumbs
pinch of sugar and nutmeg	oil

Chop up the hard-boiled eggs fairly coarsely in a basin and add the thick butter sauce. Season to taste. Shape into balls and dip in flour, the beaten egg and then coat in breadcrumbs.

Fry in deep oil until golden-brown. Drain on kitchen paper and serve with crisp, grilled bacon rashers.

* * *

THE CHILDREN'S BIRTHDAY PARTY

sandwiches

cream horns   *jam canapés*

sponge tea cakes   *meringue gateau birthday cake*

mousse of lychees

Children's parties may not be a recognised form of sport but they certainly provide masses of exercise; in comparison, preparing a four-course dinner for ten is a rest cure.

I have been told that, nowadays, children prefer their parties to be as much like adult occasions as possible – bar the drinks. Personally, I think it is a mistake to cut out sweet food entirely – there is plenty of time for cocktail parties when the children are grown-up.

SANDWICH SUGGESTIONS

Hard-boiled egg, chopped and seasoned with peeled, thinly-sliced tomato; grated cheese and shredded lettuce; minced ham and mayonnaise, mixed to a smooth cream, with sliced tomato and watercress; thinly-sliced cucumber rolled up in brown bread and butter.

CREAM HORNS

Pre-heat oven to 220°C/425°F or gas mark 7
To make 18 cream horns:

1 lb/500 g puff pastry (for recipe, see page 224)	2 ozs/60 g jam
1 egg yolk, beaten	1 pint/60 cl double cream
1 oz/30 g caster sugar	vanilla flavouring

Roll out the puff pastry to one-fifth of an inch thick, then cut in strips ten inches long and one inch wide. Moisten the edges and fold round individual moulds, ensuring the edges overlap. Brush with egg yolk mixed with a little water and roll in caster sugar. Rinse a tin in cold water, fill with the horns and bake in the oven set at 220°C/425°F or gas mark 7 for twenty to twenty-five minutes. Leave to cool. When cold, remove the moulds and fill with jam and whipped cream, flavoured with vanilla.

JAM CANAPÉS

Pre-heat oven to 190°C/375°F or gas mark 5
To make 12 jam canapés:

½ lb/250 g puff pastry (for recipe see p. 224)	raspberry jam
caster sugar	double cream
	icing sugar

Roll out the puff pastry to one-fifth of an inch thick and sprinkle with caster sugar. Fold the square of pastry edge to edge. Press lightly with the rolling pin. Sprinkle with caster sugar and fold again. Fold again in half and press gently. Allow to stand for fifteen minutes in a cold place. Then cut the folded pastry in half-inch strips across. Stand the pastry strips on a greased tin, resting on the cut side, allowing a couple of inches between each cake. Bake for eight to ten minutes in the oven at 190°C/375°F or gas mark 5 until light brown. Reduce heat and bake for a further three or four minutes. When cold, sandwich the halves with seedless raspberry jam and cream, and sprinkle with icing sugar.

SPONGE TEA CAKES

Pre-heat oven to 190°C/375°F or gas mark 5
To make 12–18 tea cakes:

2 eggs
4 ozs/125 g caster sugar
2½ ozs/75 g butter

4 fl ozs/12 cl milk
4–5 ozs/125–150 g plain flour
a few drops of vanilla essence

For the icing:
½ lb/250 g sieved icing sugar
1 tablespoon of orange juice

1 tablespoon of lemon juice
1 tablespoon of butter

Grease bun tin, dust with just a light sprinkling of the flour. Whip the eggs and sugar until fluffy. Boil butter and milk together and whip into egg mixture. Fold in the flour and add vanilla essence. Stir until smooth. Bake in the oven at 190°C/375°F or gas mark 5 for ten to fifteen minutes. Allow to cool.

To make the icing, mix with the sieved icing sugar the orange and lemon juice until all lumps have vanished. Add the butter and heat mixture very gently, stirring quickly, until the butter is absorbed. Spread mixture over the cakes with a palette knife.

MERINGUE GÂTEAU BIRTHDAY CAKE

Pre-heat oven to 190°C/375°F or gas mark 5
To make 1 × 12-inch/30-cm cake

4 eggs
8 ozs/250 g caster sugar
4 ozs/125 g plain flour
1 oz/30 g cornflour
2 teaspoons of baking powder

2 egg whites
4 ozs/125 g caster sugar
½ pint/30 cl whipped cream
redcurrant jelly
cherries

Beat the eggs and sugar for twenty minutes, or ten with an electric mixer. Add the flour and cornflour, sieved with the baking powder, and stir well. Fill a large cake tin with the mixture and bake for twenty to thirty minutes in the oven at 190°C/375°F or gas mark 5. Turn on to a wire tray to cool.

To make the meringues, whip the egg whites stiffly and fold in the sugar. With a tablespoon, set out neat blobs of the mixture on to a greased and floured tin. Bake the meringues in a very low oven for two or three hours or until a very pale fawn colour. Press lightly with the thumb to make a small hollow.

Cut the cooled cake in half and spread with a layer of redcurrant jelly and cream. Put the two halves together and cover the top with another layer of redcurrant jelly and cream. Decorate by piping on the rest of the cream and distributing the meringues and some cherries.

MOUSSE OF LYCHEES

1 large tin of lychees
vanilla essence
1 tablespoon of gelatine
2 tablespoons of caster sugar

½ pint/30 cl double cream
whipped cream and pistachio
  nuts, to garnish

Drain and chop the fruit, removing the stones. Place in individual glasses. Heat the syrup from the tin, add the vanilla and dissolve the gelatine and sugar. When cold, whip the double cream and fold in. Pour over the fruit and allow to set. Garnish with whipped cream and chopped nuts.

Menu Suggestions

DINNER AT EIGHT . . . AND YOU COULD SET YOUR CLOCK BY THE QUEEN'S appearance at the dinner table with her guests. This punctuality, I am sure, was dictated by a natural consideration for the people who worked for her. Dinner at eight meant that on a good day I could be finished in the kitchen by 10 p.m. I always saw the dinner through, right down to the serving of the coffee, although I did not, of course, have to wash up. After this I would go to my room and write out the menus for the following day. Oddly enough, this was often my greatest headache. The menus had to be in French and being no scholar of languages I used to struggle for hours with the language of haute cuisine. Eventually I found a wonderful, but very expensive, book which contained all the terms I needed, though I was still conscious of the odd mistake. However, the Queen, who speaks excellent French, was very kind about this and tactfully ignored any errors.

On special occasions I would make a list of initial suggestions and the Queen or Queen Mother would select the final dishes very carefully. We had some fairly simple menus at Clarence House but also some very grand ones. I enjoyed doing both.

People often ask me if I was made nervous by the illustrious names on the guest lists when I was cooking at Clarence House. Well, I would have been of course if I had known beforehand who was to be there. But often the Comptroller's guest list, issued a fortnight in advance, simply stated the number of guests to a particular meal. Once there were four Queens to lunch! Luckily, I did not know until afterwards when I received a message that the royal ladies had thoroughly enjoyed my sole Véronique. Had I known, I might have been influenced to try something grander. Yet sole Véronique at its best, is certainly a dish to set before a Queen.

Cooking for royalty is an honour, but it is no use pretending that the work in a royal household is not demanding. It would be easy if all one had to do was to produce inspired menus for royalty and bask in the glory of them all. But real life in royal households is not like that. In my time at Clarence House there were between eighty and a hundred *un*royal mouths to feed as well. Most lunch times I had to work to three different menus. First, the nursery, whose menus were simple but needed careful preparation. Then the royal lunch, usually with guests. Next the staff, who ate substantially from a different menu. There were also the ever-hungry policemen who ate after the staff and enjoyed whatever was going.

This chapter contains the dinner party menus I have designed and cooked over the years and which have received the most favourable comment. Some of these may suit you; some of course may not. They are not, after all, meant to be strictly adhered to. My aim is for them to inspire you with ideas of your own.

Use the menus according to your own taste, means and entertaining needs. The one thing the dishes have in common is that not only do they taste exceptionally delicious but they *look* so very attractive too. Small details like the way vegetables are served are, I think, extremely important when entertaining. Creamed spinach in little puff pastry cases, for example, is probably something you would not dream of serving up for the family, but what a difference it would make to any dinner party menu.

All of the recipes are given elsewhere in the book under the relevant chapter heading. These dinner party menus have happy memories for me. I hope you will enjoy using them, too.

MENU ONE (*serves 6*)

Consommé en Gelée aux Sherry

*

Filet de Sole Meunière
Roast Duckling
Bouchées aux Epinard
New Potatoes

*

Hot Grapefruit Salad
Poires Maraschino aux Ananas
Almond Biscuits

MENU TWO (*serves 6*)

Cold Cherry Soup Chantilly

*

Filet de Boeuf with Sauce Piquant
Potatoes Suédoise
Tomates Farcie
Salade Princesse

*

Peach Meringue with Vanilla Cream

MENU THREE (*serves 4*)

Consommé Contessa

*

Saumon Court Bouillon
Sauce Hollandaise
New Potatoes with Dill
Cucumber Salad

*

Lamb Noisettes
Champignons
Petits Pois à la Français

*

Melon Surprise

MENU FOUR (*serves 6*)

Potage Alexandra

*

Chicken Sauté Provençale
Braised Celery
Cocotte Potatoes in Tomatoes

*

Salade Alma

*

Crêpes Suzettes à la Suédoise

MENU FIVE (*serves 6*)

Baked Avocado Pear

*

Schnitzel de Veau au Diplomat
Brussels Sprouts
Macrée Potatoes
Tomato Salad with Chives

*

Crème à la Duchesse with Strawberry Sauce

MENU SIX *(serves 6)*

Asparagus in Mousseline Sauce

*

Turbot Café de Paris

*

Glazed Carré de Porc
Boiled Rice
French Beans
Watercress
Orange Sauce

*

Muscat Grapes en Gelée

Sauces and Essential Mixtures

THERE IS ONLY ONE WAY TO MAKE A GOOD SAUCE AND THAT IS WITH love and care. All sauces should have one thing in common, and that is that they should look good enough to eat by themselves.

Sauces are a versatile accompaniment to so many dishes. They can be used to harmonise with or enhance the flavour of a certain food, or they can provide a pleasant contrast. However, never try disguising indifferent food with a highly-flavoured sauce.

Of all the members of the Royal Family, the Queen Mother was perhaps the most appreciative of a good sauce, frequently sending messages of thanks and mentioning the sauce by name. In fact, I think it was my sauces that won her over, for when I first started cooking for Her Majesty at Clarence House, after Princess Elizabeth became Queen and moved to Buckingham Palace, I was naturally employed on a temporary basis only, to see how we would get along together. I understood perfectly the reasons for this since in those days all the really big kitchens were run by men, as it was thought that the administrative work of a large kitchen with a big staff was probably better handled by a man. The Queen Mother and Princess Margaret had a larger staff than that of the Queen and her family, all of whom I had to cook for as well; also, the Queen Mother and Princess Margaret frequently entertained separately, sometimes on the same day.

So if the Queen Mother was doubtful, I was certainly extremely apprehensive, but I am pleased to say that rapport was soon established – in no small way, I am sure, due to the quality and range of my sauces.

BASIC BÉCHAMEL SAUCE

1 oz/30 g butter
1 oz/30 g plain flour
$\frac{3}{4}$ pint/40 cl warm milk

pepper, salt and sugar to taste
pinch of nutmeg

This is the sauce that no cook can do without for long; it is one that never changes and that, at the same time, no two people ever make in quite the same way. The order in which the ingredients are added, the small variations of quantity, the heat of the stove, and the amount of time spent in cooking it, plus the mood of the cook, are the factors which make the classic béchamel sauce what it is. "Thick and lumpy – hot and grumpy," I always think to myself when tasting the wrong sort of béchamel, made, I am sure, in the wrong frame of mind. The right sort of béchamel must be made smoothly and sweetly, as though without a care in the world. If the telephone rings – one does not answer it.

This is how I like to make my béchamel – with a little cold butter added at the end to give a smooth consistency.

Melt half the butter, add the flour and stir over a low heat. Do not allow to brown. Add the warmed milk gradually, whisking all the time until smooth and creamy. Boil for about five or six minutes. Add the seasoning, the pinch of nutmeg and simmer for a couple of minutes. Remove from heat and stir in the rest of the butter.

MORNAY SAUCE

½ pint/30 cl béchamel sauce
1 tablespoon of grated Gruyère
    cheese
1 tablespoon of grated
    Parmesan cheese
knob of butter

Heat the béchamel sauce and stir in the grated cheese. Remove from heat and stir in the knob of butter.

SUPRÈME SAUCE (for boiled chicken)

½ pint/30 cl béchamel sauce
1 glass of dry white wine or ¼
    pint/15 cl chicken stock
pinch of garlic salt
pepper, salt and sugar to taste
1 egg yolk
1 tablespoon of double cream

Bring béchamel sauce to the boil, add the wine or stock and seasonings and simmer for five minutes. Stir in the egg yolk, remove from heat and stir in the cream.

When using with boiled chicken, first remove the skin of the chicken and allow the sauce to settle in the pan for a few minutes away from the heat. Then coat the chicken with the sauce.

SCOTCH EGG SAUCE

¾ pint/40 cl béchamel sauce
3 hard-boiled eggs

2 tablespoons of butter
salt and pepper

Make the béchamel sauce rather thin. Separate the hard-boiled egg yolks from the whites. Cut the whites in strips and sieve the yolks. Add sieved yolks and butter to the béchamel sauce and stir well over a low heat. Season to taste and add the egg whites. Serve hot.

HOLLANDAISE SAUCE

4 tablespoons of dry white
  wine or 3 tablespoons of
  white vinegar
½ teaspoon of salt

½ teaspoon of white pepper
  (preferably Mignonette)
3 egg yolks
½ lb/250 g butter
juice of ½ lemon

Hollandaise sauce, simplified here as much as possible, likes a regular low heat. Sauces made from butter and thickened with egg yolks are not designed to be served piping hot.

Put the wine or vinegar into a saucepan with five tablespoons of water and seasoning, and reduce to half the amount by boiling down. Whisk the egg yolks in a basin with three tablespoons of water and add to the sauce. Stir over a low heat until thickened. Remove from heat and add the slightly softened butter a little at a time with a small amount of water, then add the lemon juice.

Serve with vegetables – delicious with asparagus – and fish.

BÉARNAISE SAUCE

3 tablespoons of dry white
  wine or 2 tablespoons of
  malt vinegar
2 tablespoons of water
sprig of parsley
2½ tablespoons of chopped
  onion

½ teaspoon of white pepper
  (preferably Mignonette)
1 tablespoon of tomato purée
salt and cayenne pepper
1 level tablespoon of finely-
  chopped fresh parsley
3 egg yolks
6–7 ozs/175–200 g soft butter

Put the white wine (or vinegar), 2 tablespoons of water, the sprig of parsley, onion and white pepper into a saucepan and boil down to a third of the quantity. Strain and allow to cool a little.

Return to a low heat and add the tomato purée, salt, cayenne pepper and chopped parsley. Add the egg yolks one at a time, whisking continuously. Be very careful at this stage not to boil the mixture. Whisk until it becomes frothy. Remove the saucepan from the heat and add the soft butter a little at a time, still whisking. Sample the sauce for seasoning, return to a low heat and when warm, remove to a *bain marie* or double boiler. Very, very gradually, drop by drop, add 1 tablespoon of cold water.

Serve with steaks and grills.

MOUSSELINE SAUCE

3 egg yolks
pinch of salt

¼ lb/125 g soft butter

Whisk the egg yolks, 2 tablespoons of water and a pinch of salt together over a low heat until frothy. Remove from the heat and add the butter in small portions. Serve at once.

This is a light and delicate sauce, delicious with asparagus, artichokes or broccoli.

MAYONNAISE

4 egg yolks

½ teaspoon (or more, according to taste) of dry mustard

½ teaspoon of salt

1½ pints/90 cl olive or nut oil

1 tablespoon of vinegar (best malt wine or tarragon)

juice of ½ lemon

boiling water ready to drip in if necessary

dash of cayenne pepper

½ teaspoon of sugar

Mayonnaise is the basis of many sauces. You will find it very useful to have some home-made mayonnaise in stock to which you can add other ingredients to make a variety of delicious sauces. Remember when making the mayonnaise that all the ingredients must be the same temperature, so stand them all together in the same place for several hours before mixing.

Mix egg yolks, mustard and salt together into a thick paste. Add the oil, drop by drop, ensuring that each drop is whisked in and emulsifies with the paste. When the mixture is good and thick, add the vinegar drop by drop. Continue whisking all the time, alternating drops of vinegar and lemon juice with the oil. If the mixture gets stiffer than desired, soften with a few drops of boiling water. If it curdles, i.e. separates, put an extra egg yolk in another bowl and gradually whisk the curdled mixture into the new egg yolk. Finish off by adding the cayenne pepper and sugar and give a final whisk.

GREEN TARTARE SAUCE

small bunch of parsley

½ pint/30 cl mayonnaise

1 tablespoon of chopped celery

1 tablespoon of chopped chives

1 tablespoon of chopped capers

1 tablespoon of chopped dessert apple

Rinse the parsley and chop very finely. Put into a muslin bag and wring out the juice into the mayonnaise. Add all the other ingredients and mix well together. Keep the parsley for decorating.

VINAIGRETTE SALAD SAUCE WITH EGGS

½ teaspoon of dry mustard   4 hard-boiled eggs
2 tablespoons of vinegar   2 egg yolks
pepper, salt and sugar to taste   4 fl ozs/10 cl double cream

Mix the mustard with the vinegar, pepper, salt and sugar to a smooth paste. Sieve the hard-boiled egg yolks into a basin, blend in the raw egg yolks and stir well. Add the vinaigrette sauce to the egg mixture gradually, stirring all the time. Finish with the cream.

COOKED SALAD CREAM

4 tablespoons of plain flour   ½ teaspoon of sugar
1 tablespoon of mustard   2 egg yolks
½ teaspoon of salt   4 tablespoons of oil
dash of cayenne pepper

Salad cream is very quick and easy to make at home and you can make it for a fraction of the shop price.

Mix the flour and mustard with 1 pint/60 cl of water to a smooth consistency and bring to the boil. Whisk and add seasoning. Remove from heat and allow to cool a little, then add beaten egg yolks and finally stir in the oil.

BREAD SAUCE

¼ pint/15 cl milk   6 ozs/175 g fresh white
1 medium-size onion, finely-   breadcrumbs
   chopped,   ½ oz/15 g butter
2 or 3 cloves   ¼ pint/15 cl single cream
                                    pepper, salt and nutmeg

Boil the milk with the onion and cloves for five or six minutes. Remove the cloves and add the breadcrumbs. Simmer for five minutes. Then stir in the butter, cream, salt, pepper and nutmeg.

Serve with poultry and game.

The tennis party (p. 197)

ENGLISH BUTTER SAUCE

$\frac{1}{4}$ lb/125 g butter

1 oz/30 g plain flour

$\frac{3}{4}$ pint/40 cl milk

salt and pepper

pinch of nutmeg and sugar

Melt half the butter in a saucepan, add the flour and mix well over a gentle heat. Add the milk and seasoning and whisk until smooth. Simmer on a low heat for five or six minutes. Remove from the heat and add the remaining butter in small portions, stirring all the time.

The sauce should be thick and shiny and is served mainly with vegetables or fish.

HORSERADISH BUTTER SAUCE

4 ozs/125 g butter

1 tablespoon of grated horseradish

Cream the butter and mix with the grated horseradish. Do not melt the butter as this will produce the wrong sort of flavour and texture. Serve with fish.

TOMATO SAUCE

2 onions, coarsely cut

1 oz/30 g butter

6–8 tomatoes, cut up

$\frac{1}{4}$ pint/15 cl sherry

$\frac{1}{4}$ pint/15 cl water

dash of Tabasco

salt

Braise the onions in the butter and add the tomatoes. When soft add the sherry, water and a dash of Tabasco. Sample and add salt to taste. Bring to the boil and simmer for one hour with the lid on. Sieve and bring back to the boil before serving.

APPLE SAUCE

6 cooking apples

3 cloves

2 tablespoons of redcurrant jelly

pinch of salt

The children's birthday party (p. 200)

Peel, quarter and core apples and put into a saucepan with a small amount of water and the cloves. Cook for ten minutes with the lid on over a gentle heat until soft. Add the redcurrant jelly and stir well. When the apples are well pulped, sieve, put back in the saucepan and add a pinch of salt to bring out the fullness of the taste. Keep hot.

ORANGE SAUCE

juice of 3 oranges	pinch of cayenne pepper
1 tablespoon of marmalade	1 teaspoon of French mustard
1 dessertspoon of tomato sauce	1 teaspoon of cornflour

Put the orange juice, marmalade, tomato sauce, pepper and mustard into a saucepan and bring to the boil. Mix the cornflour with a little water and add, stirring all the time. Boil for one minute. Serve hot.

VANILLA SAUCE

$\frac{3}{4}$ pint/40 cl single cream	5 egg yolks
1 vanilla pod or $\frac{1}{2}$ teaspoon of vanilla essence	3 ozs/90 g caster sugar

Boil the cream with the vanilla pod for half a minute (or add vanilla essence), remove from heat, cover with a lid and stand for fifteen minutes.

Beat the egg yolks and sugar together for fifteen minutes, five minutes if you are using an electric beater. Remove the vanilla pod and add the cream to the egg mixture, whisking very hard. Pour the mixture back into the saucepan and whisk over a gentle heat until thick and frothy. Do not boil. Pour into a basin and whisk till cold.

Serve with fruit dishes, puddings, gateaux and tarts.

STRAWBERRY SAUCE

$\frac{1}{2}$ lb/250 g fresh or frozen strawberries	sugar to taste orange Curaçao

Sieve the strawberries, add sugar to taste and flavour with a little orange Curaçao. Serve with vanilla ice-cream.

BUTTERSCOTCH SAUCE

2 ozs/60 g butter
$\frac{1}{4}$ lb/125 g brown sugar
2 tablespoons of golden syrup

$\frac{1}{4}$ pint/15 cl single cream
$\frac{1}{2}$ lb/250 g caster sugar
$\frac{1}{2}$ teaspoon of vanilla essence

Mix all the ingredients together and cook slowly in the top section of a double boiler for ten minutes.

SAUCE VELOUTÉ AU CHAMPAGNE

2 ozs/60 g butter
2 oz/60 g plain flour
2 pint/60 cl good chicken or
    veal stock
salt and pepper

1 bouquet garni
1 large onion
$\frac{1}{2}$ lb/250 g mushrooms
$\frac{1}{4}$ pint/15 cl champagne or
    white wine

This is a very grand sauce that makes a banquet out of boiled chicken. The sauce can be served either separately with the chicken or the chicken meat can be flaked into the sauce to make an excellent blanquette of chicken.

Melt the butter in a saucepan, add the flour and mix well. Add the hot stock a little at a time and stir until smooth. When all the stock has been absorbed, bring to the boil. Reduce the heat and add seasoning, bouquet garni, chopped onion and mushrooms. Add the champagne and allow to simmer for half an hour. Sieve and strain the sauce.

CHAUD-FROID SAUCE

$\frac{1}{2}$ pint/30 cl double cream
$\frac{1}{2}$ pint/30 cl velouté au
    champagne sauce
    (see recipe above)

$\frac{1}{4}$ oz/8 g powdered gelatine,
    diluted in a little hot water
    or stock

Simmer the cream and velouté au champagne sauce over a gentle heat and mix in the diluted gelatine. Let the sauce cool so that it is nearly, but not quite, at setting point. Use to coat cold chicken.

THE STOCKPOT

There is some doubt these days as to whether the ever-simmering stockpot on the kitchen stove is still an essential part of the contemporary scene. Certainly it makes for a steamy kitchen and you may get fed up with the smell. Also, there is competition in the form of so many good manufactured bouillon cubes which you can buy in the specific flavour you want. However, the good cubes are quite expensive and nobody, I hope, would think of throwing away chicken and beef bones with all the goodness there waiting to be extracted. The ingredients of your stockpot will depend on what is available in your kitchen, and the season of the year.

MEAT STOCK

shin of beef	peppercorns
veal and beef bones	chicken or game carcasses
carrots	onions
parsley	thyme
bay leaf	swede
celery	1 beetroot

This is a recipe for a meat stock that leans on the side of perfection, but shows the basic method. No exact quantities can be given.

Brown the shin of beef and the bones in the oven or pan, put in a large saucepan and cover with water. Bring slowly to the boil and skim. Simmer slowly for several hours. Then strain off the bones, clean the pan and add the vegetables and herbs to the meat stock. Simmer for a further hour. Strain before using.

No salt is added until the stock is used in conjunction with a specific dish. The object is not to have a highly-flavoured liquid, but a basic stock full of goodness yet flexible enough to combine with other ingredients. To strengthen the flavour, simply reduce by boiling down in an open pan. This stock can be kept in a cold larder for anything up to a week.

FISH STOCK

to every 1 lb/500 g of fish or fish trimmings take	½ bay leaf
1½ pints/90 cl water	2 cloves
½ teaspoon of pepper	1 onion
(preferably Mignonette)	1 stick of celery
1 bouquet of parsley	1 carrot

Fish stock is the essential basis of all fish soups. The fish used for making the stock must be fresh and of good quality. Cod or haddock will do; a mixture of mussels, oysters and flat fish (sole or whiting are best) makes a stock fit for a Queen. Cooking time should be as short as possible, as the stock may take on a bitter flavour if overcooked.

Rinse and clean the fish, cut in thick slices and add the water, seasoning, herbs and vegetables to the pan. Place on a low heat and bring to the boil. Simmer until the fish is broken up. Remove at once and strain through a fine sieve, lined with dampened muslin.

You now have a good fish stock. It can be thickened by adding whipped egg or grated Gruyère or Parmesan cheese, or purée of vegetables. Flavour by adding white wine, a good branded fish soup, or lobster, oysters, shrimps etc.

ASPIC

Now that all the hard work has been taken out of aspic preparations – you used to have to boil calves' feet for hours or soak leaves of gelatine – it has once again become very popular for cold food preparation. Nobody can go wrong with the packets of easily-dissolved powdered gelatine. You simply follow the directions, using ½ oz/15 g of gelatine powder to 1 pint/60 cl of liquid. But as the aspic must taste as good as it looks, it is advisable to add your own flavouring to the mixture. For meat or fish aspic, a glass of wine can be added. For fruit jellies, first dissolve the powder in a cup of boiling water then make up to the required quantity with fruit juice.

Here are a few do's and don'ts concerning the use of aspic jelly:

1. Never boil an aspic mixture. Always dissolve the gelatine in a cupful

or more of boiling liquid first, adding afterwards the rest of the liquid which can be cold. Stir well.

2. When making a fruit, vegetable or meat mould, let the gelatine mixture thicken to the consistency of an unbeaten egg, then add the ingredients and gelatine in alternate layers.

3. To line a mould pour in some cool aspic and turn the mould round and round with smooth, steady movements so that the sides are coated first. Continue this process so that the sides and then the bottom are coated with a good layer of gelatine.

4. To decorate a mould with appropriate garnishes, like sliced, hard-boiled egg, truffle or artistic bits of flower-shaped vegetables, arrange the garnishes on top of the turned-out mould and spoon a little nearly-set aspic on top of them to hold the shape.

5. To turn out a mould, dip quickly into hot water several times, taking care that the water does not come over the top; put a plate on top of the mould, turn it upside down and shake gently. If the mould does not slide out, dip it quickly into hot water once again.

PANADE

This is a thick paste of bread and milk to which minced meat or fish is added to make a forcemeat.

Cut white bread into cubes and soak in warm milk to soften. Work with a wooden spoon until the bread has absorbed the liquid. Add salt and pepper and put the mixture over a low heat to get hot. Work with a spoon until it leaves the side of the pan. Allow it to cool before using.

FARCIE (or forcemeat)

This is a stuffing of finely-minced or sieved ingredients bound with egg and well seasoned. It should have a creamy consistency and lends flavour and bulk to other foods. Here is a recipe for fish farcie, which is normally used for stuffing salmon and trout or is rolled up inside fillets of white fish.

FISH FARCIE (or fish cream)

1 lb/500 g fillets of lemon sole,
haddock or pike
3 ozs/90 g butter
1 oz/30 g plain flour

½ pint/30 cl single cream
3 eggs, separated
salt and pepper
pinch of sugar

Pass the fish, together with the butter, through the mincer three times. In another bowl stir the flour into the cream and mix in the yolks of eggs. Season and add to the fish in small quantities, stirring to a smooth cream. Whip the whites of eggs and fold into the farcie. Use for stuffing fish.

PASTRY

One of the basic mixtures in the kitchen is pastry. Some people find it difficult to make a good, light, crunchy pastry crust, whereas others produce the most delicious pastry every time. However, don't despair. The important thing is to hit upon a good formula and once you have achieved that, go on using it until it becomes second nature.

If you have not already discovered your secret formula, the following methods for pastry may suit you. I must admit that my pastry does turn out very well – here's hoping my recipes will do the same for you too.

SHORT PASTRY

Sweet pastry for flans
To make 1 lb/500 g pastry, enough for two × 8-inch/20-cm flans:

1 oz/30 g Trex
10 ozs/300 g plain flour
rind and juice of ½ lemon

1 tablespoon of sugar
pinch of salt
3 tablespoons of iced water

Rub the fat into the flour until the mixture has a coarse, crumbly texture, and add the grated rind, the lemon juice, the sugar and the salt. Stir in the water, mix to a firm dough and let it stand for half an hour. Grease two 8-inch/20-cm flan tins, roll out the pastry to about the thickness of ¼ inch/5 mm and line the tins. Prick the pastry at the bottom of the tins, cover with rice paper to keep from rising and bake in the oven at 180°C/350°F or gas mark 4 for fifteen to twenty minutes.

Sweet pastry for fruit pies
To make 1 lb/500 g pastry, enough for two × 8-inch/20-cm flans:

4 ozs/125 g butter	2 ozs/60 g ground almonds
2 ozs/60 g sugar	(optional)
1 egg	6 ozs/175 g plain flour

Cream the butter for three minutes with 1 oz/30 g of the sugar until light and fluffy. Add the egg and mix well. Add the almonds and flour and make into a firm paste on a floured board. Allow to stand for half an hour. Roll out and sprinkle with sugar. Fold the dough into a ball, then roll again and bake in the oven at 180°C/350°F or gas mark 4 for about twenty to thirty minutes.

Short pastry for meat pies
To make 12 oz/350 g pastry, enough for two × 8-inch/20-cm pie lids:

3 ozs/90 g butter	pinch of salt
1 oz/30 g lard	1 tablespoon of water
8 ozs/250 g plain flour	1 egg

Rub the butter and lard into the flour and salt, stir in the water and egg and mix to a thin dough. Cover a dish of cooked meat and bake in the oven at 180°C/350°F or gas mark 4 for thirty to thirty-five minutes.

PUFF PASTRY

To make 2 lbs/1 Kg of pastry:

1 lb/500 g plain flour	1 lb/500 g butter
pinch of salt	½ pint/30 cl cold water

Sieve flour and salt into a large basin. Rub in 4 ozs/125 g of butter and mix until fine and crumbly. Make a well in the centre and pour in the water a little at a time, mixing gently until the mixture becomes a stiff dough. Form into a ball and allow to stand for fifteen minutes in a cool place. Knead remaining butter until soft and make into a flat, round cake. Roll out the pastry so that it is a little thicker in the middle than at the sides and place the butter in the middle. Fold the pastry over the pat of butter like a parcel and put in a cold place for ten minutes. Roll out the pastry into a square about ¾ inch/20 mm thick and fold the two sides to meet in the middle, then fold in half. Roll out into a square again and repeat the folding process four times. Rest the pastry for twenty minutes and again roll out and repeat the folding process. Again roll four times and rest the pastry. Repeat twice more and rest the pastry for one hour before rolling out for use in pies or bouchées. Bake in the oven at 220°C/425°F or gas mark 7 for the first ten minutes. For pies that need a full half an hour's cooking, reduce the heat for the remainder of the time.

SUET CRUST

1½ lb/750 g plain flour
½ teaspoon of salt
1 teaspoon of baking powder

5 ozs/150 g shredded beef suet
¼ pint/15 cl water

Sieve the flour, salt and baking powder into a basin, mix in the suet, make a well and pour in warm water. Mix to a fairly stiff dough. Grease a 2 pint/125 cl pudding basin and roll out the dough. First of all, line the basin with the dough, leaving some of the paste hanging over the sides of the basin. Put in the filling. Cover the top with the extra paste rolled out in a circle to fit. Press the top firmly into position and trim off the edges close to the basin. Cover the pudding with a cloth, greaseproof paper or foil, fasten with string and put in a saucepan with boiling water to come half way up the pudding basin. Steam according to the time given in the particular recipe you are using – usually from four to six hours.

Note If making a sweet pudding instead of savoury, substitute one teaspoon of sugar for the half teaspoon of salt in the above list of quantities.

The Settings

LISTED BELOW ARE THE NAMES OF TABLEWARE, GLASSWARE AND cutlery, kindly lent to the publishers by Harrods Ltd and Mappin & Webb Ltd for use in the colour plates:

Fillet of beet with mushrooms and Yorkshire pudding (frontispiece): Crown Derby Duesbury Border tableware, Mappin & Webb claret jug and sauce boat, Royal Brierley vase; Consommé ris de veau au petits pois vert (opposite p. 24): Royal Albert bone china, plain white fluted with gold band, Mappin & Webb Olympic silverware; Cold consommé with oysters (opposite p. 25): Royal Worcester plain white with gold band tableware, Mappin & Webb Esperia silverware; Velouté de volaille froid (opposite p. 36): Paragon Innocence tableware, Mappin & Webb Pembury silverware; Coquilles St Jacques Balmoral (between p. 36 and p. 37): Royal Worcester tableware, plain white with gold band and scallop shells, Mappin & Webb Athenian silverware; Roulades de saumon fumée (between p. 36 and p. 37): Spode Trade Winds tableware, Mappin & Webb Featheredge silverware; Saumon court bouillon (opposite p. 37): Royal Doulton Belmont tableware; Salmon trout farcie in aspic (opposite p. 48): Mappin & Webb silver platter and ice bucket, Royal Brierley glass posy bowl; Lobster in aspic (opposite p. 49): Spode Sheffield tableware, Mappin & Webb silver vase; Lobster thermidor (opposite p. 60): Minton Buckingham tableware, Royal Brierley Princess glassware, Mappin & Webb Olympic silverware; Fillet of Dover sole Regina (between p. 60 and p. 61): Minton Buckingham tableware, Mappin & Webb silver vase; Turbot Café de Paris (between p. 60 and p. 61): Minton Imperial Gold tableware, Mappin & Webb candlestick; Entrecôte grill à la Bolognese (opposite p. 61): Royal

Doulton Empress tableware, Mappin & Webb Pembury silverware; Filet mignon Arenburg (opposite p. 72): Minton Stanwood tableware, Royal Brierley glass vase, Mappin & Webb Pembury silverware; Marinaded beef roulades (opposite p. 73): Minton Consort tableware, Mappin & Webb Rat Tail silverware, Royal Brierley glassware: Pink beef (opposite p. 84): Mappin & Webb silver platter, Mappin & Webb Pembury carving knife and fork, Royal Doulton Sarabande vegetable dish, Royal Brierley salad bowl; Navarin of lamb (between p. 84 and p. 85): Royal Doulton Clarendon tableware, Mappin & Webb Olympic silverware; Grilled lamb cutlets with parsley butter and purée of green peas (between p. 84 and p. 85): Crown Derby Duesbury Border tableware, Royal Brierley glass salad bowl, Mappin & Webb Louis XVI silverware; Lamb noisettes (opposite p. 85): Royal Doulton Clarendon tableware, Mappin & Webb Olympic cutlery; Glazed saddle of veal (opposite p. 96): Spode Indigo Blue tableware, Royal Brierley glassware, Mappin & Webb Louis XVI silverware; Sauté of veal with artichoke hearts (opposite p. 97): Royal Doulton Rennaissance tableware; Fricandeau of veal (opposite p. 108): Paragon Harmony tableware; Cutlets de veau with spaghetti (between p. 108 and p. 109): Royal Brierley glassware, Mappin & Webb Athenian silverware, Royal Doulton Sarabande tableware; Escalops of pork with cream sauce (between p. 108 and p. 109): Royal Doulton Vanborough tableware; Glazed carré de porc with orange sauce (opposite p. 109): Spode Sheffield silverware, Mappin & Webb sauce boat, Mappin & Webb Kings Pattern carving knife and fork; Chicken chaud-froid (opposite p. 120): Mappin & Webb silver platter, Mappin & Webb Athenian salad servers, Royal Brierley posy bowl; Chicken sauté (between p. 120 and p. 121): Minton Grasmere tableware, Mappin & Webb Esperia silverware; Cutlets de poulet sauté (between p. 120 and p. 121): Royal Doulton Sarabande tableware, Royal Brierley glassware, Paul Lamerie silverware; Poussins with pommes au gratin (opposite p. 121): Minton Grasmere tableware, Mappin & Webb silverware; Pheasant pie (opposite p. 144): Royal Doulton Sarabande, Mappin & Webb silver candlestick; Stuffed partridge (between p. 144 and p. 145): Minton Imperial Gold tableware, Royal Brierley glassware, Mappin & Webb Athenian silverware; Roast grouse (between p. 144 and p. 145): Royal Doulton Belmont tableware, Royal Brierley salad bowl, Mappin & Webb vase; Terrine of game (opposite p. 145): Minton Buckingham tableware;

Turkey with walnut stuffing (opposite p. 156): Royal Derby Panel (Green) tableware, Mappin & Webb silver platter, Mappin & Webb Athenian carving knife and fork; Asparagus in mousseline sauce (between p. 156 and p. 157): Royal Doulton Platinum Concord tableware; Vanilla soufflé (between p. 156 and p. 157): Spode Fleur de Lys tableware, Mappin & Webb silverware; Banana-filled meringues in candied syrup (opposite p. 157): Royal Doulton Canton tea set, Mappin & Webb Laurel and Ribbon silverware; Summer pudding (opposite p. 168): Worcester Regency Ruby tableware, Mappin & Webb Athenian silverware; Baked Alaska (opposite p. 169): Mappin & Webb silverware, Royal Brierley glass fruit bowl; Crème à la reine (opposite p. 180): Royal Brierley glass bowl, Mappin & Webb sauce boat, Mappin & Webb Chesterfield serving spoon; Crème marron (between p. 180 and p. 181): Mappin & Webb silver platter, Paul Lamerie serving spoon; Baked comice pears (between p. 180 and p. 181): Minton Bellemeade tableware, Mappin & Webb Pembury silverware, Royal Brierley glassware; Crème à la duchesse (opposite p. 192): Minton Avonlea tableware; Poires Maraschino aux ananas (opposite p. 193): Royal Doulton Alton tableware; The tennis party (opposite p. 216): Royal Doulton Alton tableware, Mappin & Webb silverware; The children's birthday party (opposite p. 217): Royal Doulton Bunnykins tableware.

Index